The Winter Sun

Also by Fanny Howe

ESSAYS

The Wedding Dress: Meditations on Word and Life
The Lives of a Spirit / Glasstown: Where Something Got Broken
The Needle's Eye: Passing through Youth

POETRY

Eggs
Poem from a Single Pallet
Robeson Street
The Vineyard
Introduction to the World
The Quietist
The End
O'Clock
One Crossed Out
Selected Poems
Gone
Tis of Thee
On the Ground
The Lyrics
Come and See
Second Childhood

FICTION

Forty Whacks
First Marriage
Bronte Wilde
Holy Smoke
In the Middle of Nowhere
The Deep North
Famous Questions
Saving History
Nod
Indivisible
Economics
Radical Love: Five Novels

The Winter Sun

Notes on a Vocation

Fanny Howe

Graywolf Press

Publication of this volume is made possible in part by a grant provided by the Minnesota State Arts Board, through an appropriation by the Minnesota State Legislature; a grant from the Wells Fargo Foundation Minnesota; and a grant from the National Endowment for the Arts, which believes that a great nation deserves great art. Significant support has also been provided by the Bush Foundation; Target; the McKnight Foundation; and other generous contributions from foundations, corporations, and individuals. To these organizations and individuals we offer our heartfelt thanks.

Published by Graywolf Press
250 Third Avenue North, Suite 600
Minneapolis, Minnesota 55401
All rights reserved.

www.graywolfpress.org

Published in the United States of America

ISBN 978-1-55597-520-3

4 6 8 9 7 5 3

Library of Congress Control Number: 2008935600

Cover design: Jeenee Lee Design

Cover and interior art: Rachel Melis

To my sisters

"Dear Child, I also by pleasant Streams
Have wander'd all Night in the Land of Dreams;
But tho' calm & warm the waters wide,
I could not get to the other side."

"Father, O father! What do we here
In this land of unbelief and fear?
The Land of Dreams is better far,
Above the light of the Morning Star."

—WILLIAM BLAKE

Contents

A Vocation 3

The Message 9

Branches 13

America 57

Person, Place, and Time 61

Waters Wide 155

The Chosen 181

The Land of Dreams 185

Evocation 189

The Winter Sun

A Vocation

Since early adolescence I have wanted to live the life of a poet. What this meant to me was a life outside the law; it would include disobedience and uprootedness. I would be at liberty to observe, drift, read, travel, take notes, converse with friends, and struggle with form.

Struggling with form meant creating problems of self-expression that only I could solve. This required boundless time, no obligations, lots of conversation and love, little money, little stability but always freedom to play with sound and meaning. I was surrounded by poetry at home so this should have been easy, but another atmosphere undermined its powers.

Like the rest of my generation, I was catapulted into a double bind. On the one hand each of us was valued, treated to an education in humanist values, and nourished for a long life; on the other hand we were told to hide under our desks during nuclear bomb alerts, and to wait there in the knowledge that we were as disposable as pieces of tissue paper that could blow away like ashes.

While we learned languages, poetry, science, and athletics, the prevailing social attitude was nihilist. Not officially so, not with reference to Nietzsche, but in the stirring cavities of decision making and imagination. Mass murder, global destruction, and genocide were idle topics. We grew up at the tail end of the Victorian period and at the beginning of the postmodern. In the year 1968 the contradictory forces behind the Vietnam War and the civil rights movement came to a head and my generation embodied the conflict and attempted to find synthesis and progress.

Now the millennium has come and gone and I am in a hermitage facing a field of snow and bristling grain where there is a line of gray trees at the end. The sky has the wintry golden blush that makes it seem to swell like water. I hear cars and trucks in the distance. Over the years I have written during days just like these, when there was snow, or cold, and some sense of safety and enclosure. More often I have written on the road in the middle of children, crowds at train stations, airports, motels, bus depots, in offices and schoolyards.

I have put this collection on the table in order to discover what I was doing during those times, because it was not just a matter of writing poems. That activity was inseparable from the dialectical questions of my generation, from the paradoxes of a life spent in a cynical social terrain.

Why was I chained to these language problems that I myself had created? Why all this scratching and erasing? It was more like drawing an invisible figure than painting what was in front of me. I wanted something to recognize: a disembodied presence.

A friend wrote down some words for me shortly before he died: "Poetry is backwards logic. You can't write poetry unless you have knowledge of, or taste for, this 'backwards' way of finding truth."

Another person said sound is eternal, it has no beginning. And a Hindu teacher said to me, "The Upanishads were never written for the first time."
I am always wondering at the way there are varieties of points of view, just as there are different names for the same things and concepts.

This collection of notes and memories is an effort to resolve the question: What was this strange preoccupation that seemed to have no motive, cause, or final goal and preceded all that writing that I did. Did it begin in the environment of childhood, or was it formed out of alien properties later? If I had known what I was doing all along, would I have done it? What people, places, books, and things guided me? What could I call what was calling me?

A vocation that has no name.

The Message

If you could take my hand and lead me along the streets and paths with your free hand outstretched and finger pointing to a future place and say, That is where we are going.
Then even if what I saw ahead was chaos and pain, I could think, There is no reason to fear after all.

If you could say, We will have to travel along separate roads battered by tumultuous weather, disappointment, starvation, hospitals, jails, and physical pain, but we are going There, to that point you see up ahead. There is where we will be together at the end.
Look. See our future, out there?

Then I would be able to say now, All will be well.

If you could say, We will rest against that building. We will die outside, there, where a solid red wall surrounds a sanctuary, as you once dreamed it would—it won't be occupied or ever have been. . . . I would be happy.

But I start down the path without you.
I am just outside a town exactly the size of a labor camp, but it has the opposite use. It is full of young people learning and living free. Prosperous, peaceful, bookish, and fresh. I am walking on a path that used to be a railroad track that ran to the town.

It is winter. Branches are broken, trees cracked by a recent ice storm. I cross over a bridge. On the right and below, where the river flooded and now is thick and iced, I see a deer hanging over the branch of a tree.

Velvety, frozen, not even the birds have set to eating it. The deer hangs like the fate of childhood among the branches and snow.

Everything has already happened at every step I take. I enter, with each move, the past of the place I am entering. This would be true on a city street, with people walking toward me. I would be entering the face of their past, they would be entering mine. Everything would be over for all of us everywhere we stepped.

If you could say, That is the future. Up that road where you are walking now. That is the actual future and I will meet you there.
Then I could say, Now I am safe.

But wherever I step I am stepping into a place that was just finished at the moment I arrived. If I freeze here, one foot poised to go forward, to land on the path, I will at least be living in the present and the past will know it.

But still I want you to come through the trees and say to me, Up ahead, there is the future. The place we will be together at the end, because then I would know, in the end, it all made sense.

The world's past is what stands before us and what we enter. It is as true as two plus two being four. As still and opaque as a finished painting. The bridge, the deer, the wrecked and cracked trees. A slash of red in the western sky. Which way did I forget to go? Which turn did we miss? Which bend shall I follow back?

Branches

I was born during a lunar eclipse in the fall of 1940. My father enlisted in the army when Germany declared war on America. Soon after my mother and sister and I took an overnight train from Buffalo to Boston, and moved into an apartment on Craigie Street in Cambridge. The building was within easy walking distance of Harvard Square, where our mother worked; it was made up of two large brick buildings, a weedy lot behind, and a tarmac road between. There was a small restaurant called La Cantina smelling of hot rolls in a basement space.

My sister, Susan, and I shared a room with many windows in the back of the railroad flat. She was three and a half years older than me, which would have made her six at the time. The day of my birth must have been a dark day for her, but being oblivious to that, I idolized her and happily did her bidding. We settled ourselves into the classic order determined by the superiority of the firstborn.

Cambridge was a man's world, even with many men away in the war. This fact and the omnipresent news of the battles abroad intensified the way we lived with our mother. The atmosphere was permeated with potential: every moment erupted by a hope followed by a failed hope. As if clouds were trying to form into a legible text and could not. The way we lived was in a contained routine within a natural world of great beauty, a world of literature, too, and of news from abroad. On Craigie Street there was an Episcopal convent, another apartment building, and residential houses made of wood. Every morning I went to a little day care called, oddly, Miss Scattergood's. My sister pulled me there by the hand and then she marched on to her school, Buckingham. Later I would learn that many of our playmates were children of émigré academics, sons and daughters of linguists, historians, and scientists who had fled Germany and Eastern Europe.

Every Sunday our mother dutifully transported us by subway to 16 Louisberg Square on Beacon Hill to have midday lunch with our grandfather, for whom our father was named. Our grandfather lived in a townhouse with an Irish maid who was named Mary like our Irish mother. Mary Lawrence was tucked in a bedroom behind the kitchen downstairs. Our grandfather was a portly man with a watch chain and vest, a white moustache as coarse as his hair, and the good nature ascribed to those with few doubts. He blew pipe rings and played a recorder. His mouth was the center of focus for me.

His apartment, an elegant floor-through, did not let much sun in, so only yellow lamplight spread over the tables and chairs and objects brought from China generations before. A Steinway sat near one window and there he played and sang Gilbert and Sullivan songs and favorite hymns. On those visits my sister and I were not allowed to wear dungarees or sneakers, but had to dress up, and in the cooler weather we wore matching coats and hats, navy blue with naval insignia, and were asked to march up and down saluting and singing the "Marines' Hymn" for the pleasure of our grandfather and mother. Every Sunday we had the same lunch: chicken consommé, chicken and rice, and vanilla ice cream with pie for dessert. I was terrified of making a mistake or breaking something. Water jiggled in a crystal fingerbowl beside each plate, and behind us stood a tall ivory pagoda under glass, just waiting to be smashed.

I have no memory of my sister's or mother's face during those occasions but only of the bachelor atmosphere. My grandfather was long a widower, portly, very white, mild of manner, and with a stutter that riveted me because it was as if his voice wanted to turn into a musical instrument (or song) that would take his words to another level; the fact that he dared to let his voice utter odd sounds was wonderful in the suppressed Bostonian world he inhabited. He and our mother spoke about mutual friends, family, and of course developments in the war. A bakery smell of books lingered around the shelves; some of them were for children, but they were not the ordinary American fare. These were Victorian storybooks, including pictures of curly-haired children in pinafores, stone walls, golliwogs, leaping figures with scissors following them to cut off their thumbs, and gardens containing pale but specific flowers. Our mother had these books from her own youth in Dublin, and she spoke of the same songs, poems, and novels as our grandfather did. I knew as a child that she was foreign. The reality is, they were turn-of-the-century and the aura of this time was so strong, it affected everything I did and thought about later.

☙

When I am back in Boston in 2000 a soft snow is falling diagonally. There is no wind. The trees are creamy and drooping. Even the birds are hidden away, waiting for these lazy snowdrops to stop though I hear a few chirps as if sparrows were entombed in brick.

Boston contained in its physical structures the traces of its nineteenth-century inhabitants until after the war. Even into the fifties these words about a cemetery by Henry James would apply as a metaphor for Boston:

> If, while the air is thickened by this frosty drizzle, the calendar should happen to indicate that the blessed vernal season is already six weeks old, it will be admitted that no depressing influence is absent from the scene.

Boston in my childhood had the feel of a graveyard. Epigrammatic, grim, entrenched, with avenues cut straight around the circular gardens. The river was still, except when the Harvard crew broke its surface. Compared to New York City, Boston was like a used, dropped newspaper that no one wanted to stoop to pick up. Montreal danced by comparison. Boston was not introspective but conservative, repeating Fridays at symphony and teas at the Athenaeum in a way that only outsiders would find interestingly historic. It was the arrival of the Kennedys on the political scene that took the place apart and ended that long trance. The Irish, who had provided the basic workforce for the city, were the ones who took over and brought it back to life.

As Frederick Douglass said, "The limits of tyrants are proscribed by the endurance of those whom they oppress."

The servant class, the Irish maids, cops, firemen, laborers, soldiers, all Catholics, did as they would do in Northern Ireland after the 1960s: they went to school and became professional. The other ethnic minorities in Boston fought among themselves, crowded together, or left the city. WASPs hung on, but the central division among them, between Republicans and Democrats, weakened their hold. As usual, African Americans had the hardest time in Boston, supposedly a city of integration, abolition, and liberty, and almost all the brightest of them left for New York, or left the country. In our end of town hardly any women had a job.

Day and night our mother was out at work. We had many babysitters. One had a hunchback and said her brother ran over her back on his tricycle when she was a baby. Another had a brother who raised odorless skunks on Cape Cod. And there was one who smacked my butt with the bristles of a hairbrush and whom I prayed would die, which she did almost immediately. My sister and I loved having our lively young mother at home, with the radio on, playing either the news or music that gave her pleasure and made her stride around with a glass of something strong for a partner. Friends often came over.

Our Sunday trips to see our grandfather were special because we were all out in the world together. My sister and I would huddle in the bedroom off the kitchen with Mary Lawrence, reading the Sunday comics on her bed or hearing her stories about Ireland and seeing her postcards from home that showed lambs and shamrocks. The presence of our missing father trailed us everywhere. After lunch, the three of us would walk back down Beacon Hill along Charles Street to the iron staircase going up to the elevated subway stop. Our father was the only reason we were anywhere then; and he was nowhere.

From the bridge we viewed the gray fortress of the city jail and the river flowing out to the harbor. Beacon Hill was a brick hump topped with the gold dome. When the snow came, the blood-red brick of the city grew white and the ice on the river was a stiff winding-sheet that led out to the Atlantic and across to Ireland. The sky was dramatic and emotional at every hour of the day. The war contributed to every shadow and drop; consciousness of its force was made up only of objects and loose parts, of animate and inanimate, of constant motion, wind, rain, hope, dread, and expectation.

That war was like an immense umbrella held high in the air and shadowing our every move. (Even now I can feel its shade, even if only a corner is left.) In our railroad apartment during that time the orange lightbulbs at the back of the radio burned day and night. Churchill, Hitler, Roosevelt roared through the static behind its rough-textured cover. American broadcasters' voices reported catastrophe. Music tinkled during ads and via singers, operas, symphonies played in our small living room. I confused Roosevelt with my father, because without form they seemed to be one man.

At that time I had only one memory of my father from the top of the stairs in Buffalo. He was in a uniform and he was saying a hesitant good-bye. Otherwise there were few photographs. He had left his job as dean of a new law school at Buffalo and had left behind his work on the letters and life of Oliver Wendell Holmes. He was thirty-seven. He had been to Europe only once before, as far as Ireland, where he had met his in-laws and where he vowed never to return. He was known to have a dread of travel, yet he was gone longer than most fathers.

Every evening I was put in my room to bed earlier than my sister, and in summer it was often bright still, daytime, only around five or six. There I became hypersensitive to sound, smell, image, experiencing a kind of synesthesia that held all the parts of my immediate environment together as one. The natural world was like a second skin or garment made of air and gold. Next door and out my window was an Episcopal convent, containing a few old women and a staircase with an electric chair they let me ride when I came inside.

It was through my window facing onto their house that the sun fell around the walls as a living presence that I called (secretly) God. Whether it was cold, yellow, white, warm, orange, or a spread of violet, that light was my surrounding other. I now suppose it was equivalent to the *geistige* that the philosopher Edith Stein describes as being always present to consciousness; it refused to go away, and it refused to be located. I sensed it as light with an intention infusing it, a presence that had no attributes, not even love. I breathed it and it made images emerge from inside me to meet the ones on the outside. Its attachment to me came because of my being young, and from what I could tell, it would disappear with age.

Since my relationship to others was being formed at the same time, I held myself a little apart from those who might drain this secret out of me. In these days and months of waiting for my father, I kept my anticipation to myself, it was so intense. From then on I preferred aloneness and expectation to anything else. Outside my bedroom door my mother and sister shared their passions for theater, literature, and history. This would always be the arrangement. They would be madly discussing books, because neither one was ever without one, and each shouted opinions of the utmost intensity back and forth. I was often mute in the background, sucking my thumb and daydreaming. In this posture I was conscious of being coherent inside my skin, but it would take a while before I found out that I could test this coherence to see if it could survive changes in time and space—by moving great distances.

The drama of New England weather was enough for me in those years. I pulled back my curtains or drew up the shades in the morning and the theater of the sky was in progress. Clouds of many shapes and colors raced or rolled overhead until night fell. There might have been snow in the night, or rain that formed shiny and darkened circles in the potholes and curbs. In spring and summer, honeysuckle, violets, lily of the valley, wisteria, lilacs, tulips, and daffodils bloomed in gardens up and down the streets. In fall, elderberry bushes were bright red and yellow leaves sank or slid underfoot. In winter the arms of the trees crackled inside ice sleeves or sank low to the ground. Birds raced off to the sanctuary of Mount Auburn Cemetery.

Our mother walked home, blithely alone, at midnight from her work in the Idler Club's Agassiz Theatre at Radcliffe where she directed plays. Many evenings she would have friends home and they would sit close to the hot body of the radio. When the black-outs occurred in Cambridge—practice air raids accompanied by sirens—the radio played on. We heard the recurrent names: Afrika Korps, Rommel, Ribbentrop, Molotov, Brenner Pass, Dieppe, Vichy, Mussolini. When Hitler spoke, it sounded as if the radio were breaking into static to meet his rasping voice. Didn't evil know it was evil? I wondered. An old man played a hurdy-gurdy on the streets of Cambridge all through the war. Flowers garlanded his organ. A legless beggar sat outside Woolworth's in all weather, protected by a striped awning, his board-on-wheels parked beside him and a hat for falling small change.

As I began to see injustice close up, I was filled with a desire to understand what made people who suffered for nothing want to go on living.

⚜

I look and see what has come to look back at me: a sizzle of frost links forms between the tracks and winter clouds are furry.
They shield the fields the way fresh water shields a fish.
A chill burns color from all things
While wool whirls from factory spires,
Spouts and tunnels in the air and silk ropes.
"The order of the signs"—these are called.

Perhaps the self (like smoke) is spun from infinity with every-thing else and a growing awareness of its pending annihilation. The self opens up to its condition in stages and often because of its accompanying realization of adult hypocrisy. Childhood is the stage where a person either submits to or resists life as an-other adult. Why go on to become that?

Martin Luther, in John Osborne's play, said, "I lost the body of a child, a child's body, the eyes of a child . . . and I was afraid and went back to find it . . . But I can't."

Maybe the day the self submits to its own becoming, it ties itself up into a lunglike organ where it thrashes around till the last day. All this occurs at a moment in calendar time. After that, the self is carried through libraries, museums, city parks, churches, movie theaters, dark streets, blazing sun, beds, and across oceans.

Somewhere the scholar Franz Rosenzweig wrote that "the self has no relations, cannot enter into any, and remains ever itself. Thus it is conscious of being eternal; its immortality amounts to an inability to die."

But the self that I mean can choose many ways to extend its transit through the world, and even to escape it by suicide rather than to crawl along through ordinary time. The wonderful thing is that it can also overcome these choices and stay with childhood! The child poised on the threshold of a door is also the ghost going the other way; they are one action immortalized by a single position toward the world: *not there.*

The postwar decade was not a deeply subjective time even in Cambridge. There were psychologists around and McLean Hospital, ready to catch demented professors and their children, but by and large the discourse was political and social. Literature still provided the most popular way to study the human heart and personality, and people read novels and talked about them the way they do movies now. But one would never discuss one's own motives or libido around the house. My father spoke of the attraction of suicide innumerable times, over the sink, and quoted Holmes at his most dour, as I dried the dishes. My sister and I had a skittish physical relationship to him. No touching, no embracing. Yet between us all was an electric tension as fiery as that static which ghost hunters felt between their upraised palms. He was small, he was thin, big-eared, blue-eyed, charismatic, and athletic.

⚐

The philosopher Edith Stein said that streams of consciousness are different for everyone and this is why the soul is individuated within each person. Like the sky dappling the cover of a river with refractions and reflections of all kinds, and the river keeps sliding along with its content intact. Only the quality of the sun can infiltrate the water—either a bold yellow one or a pale winter sun, or all the ones between those two in the spectrum. Now (five years ago) I am under a cold sun and watch the snow fall outside the glass like beautiful film that I am shooting with the lenses of my eyes.

⚐

During the war an American studies program was initiated at Harvard, and American literature, always belittled in relation to English and European, was given new attention. F. O. Matthiessen was particularly involved in this revival. Matthiessen was a Christian socialist—politically to the left and socially conservative. He lived with his cats on Beacon Hill, believed in God, and was a favorite at dinner parties. He helped introduce a tutorial system at Harvard that was modeled on that of English universities; he believed in the pure pursuit of wisdom rather than the accumulation of information. At the same time he was involved in the Harvard Teachers Union and was passionate on the subject of democracy. He wondered in words that now seem radically lost: "In a democracy there can be but one fundamental test of citizenship, namely: Are you using such gifts as you possess for or against the people?"

His great critical work, *American Renaissance,* was devoted to the five major male writers of the nineteenth century—Whitman, Thoreau, Hawthorne, Emerson, and Melville—not only as literary but also as political figures. The measure of a writer, for Matthiessen, was the degree of his or her commitment to the American vision of a Christian democracy. He chose Melville as the one who best understood the tragic consequences of individualism and analyzed Emerson's "will to virtue" in terms of an ominous will to conquest, and compared this to Germany. He was horrified by professionals and specialists in a growing defense industry moving onto the university grounds. He never gave up his political position.

He was a close friend of my parents' and my aunt's who sang this anonymous song to us:

> My falcon fair, I loved so dear, that home I brought the
>   treasure,
> To rest so soft, to hawk no more, for hunter's cruel pleasure.
> He quickly learned to have no fear, and my commandment
>   heeding,
> Away he flew, my falcon fair, beyond my window speeding.
>
> He westward flew; I followed fast, but all in vain I sought him.
> I heard his voice; 'twas quickly stilled. A savage eagle caught
>   him.

And I knew 'twere better far to show such kindness never,
Because I loved my falcon fair; he is lost to me forever.

⚜

In 1945, with our father still gone, I joined my sister at
Buckingham School, which was built to preserve a Victorian
English perspective on the world. Over the next few years all
of us girls studied Latin, French, and English history; we read
Jane Austen and the Lake poets. *Moby Dick* was still called "a
boy's book." In our geography classes there were maps of South
American countries, India, Africa, and Asia on which each territory was pictorially identified by its products—grain, oil, fruit,
tobacco, and so on. The irritable, aging teachers hurried us
through American history with contempt.

At home we waited for mail from our grandmother and our
uncle John in Ireland, and our father. Uncle John painted in
watercolor little images of the Irish sky: long gray blue fingers
crawling over the mountains. Our grandmother sent a bunch
of shamrock by mail once, pressed in crinkled transparent
paper; she also sent lace. Our mother stared over her typewriter
out the window at the sky. She interpreted from its weight and
texture a myriad of possible weathers, most of them bad.

She became increasingly impatient with the length of the war
and American involvement. She had a streak of Irish isolation-
ism in her, but like most people her politics were generally malleable and self-referential. She was an iconoclast for whom the
October Revolution was a peak moment in history, ushering in
one noble uprising after another. She loved it when her husband wrote home expressing sympathy for the Italian underground and the leftist resistance movements. Bernard Shaw and
Sean O' Casey were her heroes and, of course, Joyce. She played

devil's advocate and advocated insurgency. Yet she continued to long for the company of the "frozen chosen" of Boston—WASPs with money.

There were many lively dinner parties in Boston during the war when the male-female ratio was utterly out of kilter. People came to our apartment and my sister and I lay in our room and listened to the laughter down the hall while the branches scratched on our windowpanes and car lights drifted by; we identified them as fairies and gave them names. She remembered and I imagined our father, and each of us invented a male companion in those years. Susan's was an elf who lived in a mailbox and mine was a giant hunched inside a brick building on the edge of Harvard Square.

On one cold white morning in late November 1944, there was a knock on the apartment door as we three were sitting down to breakfast. A man called, "Paper!" Our mother in her nightgown went to see what he wanted, convinced it was money. When she opened the door, our father was there. Dressed in uniform, carrying an army bag and packages, he was smaller than any of us remembered. His eyes were deep set and shining, his posture soldierly, his manner shy, as he was invited into the home he had never seen.

I remember how he sat at the end of the table with a few presents spread out for each of us and how we circled him nervously, analytically. He had a little hole in one cheek from shrapnel. He had, he told us, been blown off a toilet seat by an explosion. He was home for a few days only. On December 3, Matthiessen wrote to his best friend: "Young Mark Howe (a Lieut-Colonel with AMG) is just back from France, and Helen gave a little party for him. It is fine to see a firm and resolute believer in democracy, who has been doing the best job he can."

He had to leave again for Europe, this time Potsdam, and from there to Washington. He told our outraged mother that his absence was a necessity and that "the quality of misery is probably more important than the fact of unhappiness." For him distress could be justified if the goal was good. He told his sister Helen that he had found "considerable satisfaction, with all the outward despair" in those years abroad during the war. (Later he would remark to a friend in an idyllic setting, "I wonder if I should be unhappy because I'm happy or happy because I'm unhappy.")

He would become a professor of law at Harvard and a political activist. WASP eggheads and Jewish intellectuals would take over the town, although the Square, small-town and provincial except for the Brattle Theatre, gave little sign of anything mentally exciting going on, except in the bookstores. The regular shops could be found on any Main Street. Students and professors sat around in brightly lit greasy coffee shops. An English muffin, bitter cups of coffee in thick white cups, tomato soup, and a dry sandwich on white bread. The wives stayed home and took care of the house, shopped for meat-and-potato dinners, and belonged to impromptu clubs. There was a lot of smoking and drinking. Chesterfields and cocktails. Some of the women typed up their husbands' manuscripts and in the process edited and rewrote them.

Our mother quit her job at Radcliffe and before she did anything else, she took us to Ireland. It was the summer of 1947. My sister was ten and I was six years old. The war was barely over. The three of us stayed at our grandfather's apartment on Louisberg Square deep into the night. We were laid out on sofas to wait like invalids. A taxi then took us to Boston's Logan Airport. We were photographed by a newspaperman on the tarmac on our way out to the plane. This was a human interest story: one of the first civilian flights out of Boston was taking a woman and two children to Ireland to see their grandmother.

There was a salty night breeze from Boston Harbor when we boarded the small Pan Am plane. A porthole framed the white moon swathed in clouds. On board the plane were a great many clerics and nuns and only a few civilians, no children but us. Rosaries rattled under the whisper of Hail Marys as the plane bumped along the ground to takeoff, then leaned out over the black sea. There were two rows of two seats and not very many of them. My sister and mother sat together. I was put beside a stranger for the journey because I was afraid of my sister's wrath if I begged to be beside our mother.

Retching and vomiting, bellyaching and ear-aching continued all the way to Gander in Newfoundland, where the plane was stalled for twenty-four hours, owing to engine trouble. I remember wandering among the seats full of weary travelers and speaking for a long time with a man who was trying to get to Dublin before his mother died. I was aware that my being a child was a comfort to him. The popular songs "Five Minutes More" and "I Wonder, I Wonder, I Wonder" played somewhere in the background. The remnants of the war could be seen out the windows: war planes, now useless. Gander had been a stopover point for the military throughout the war. We then flew through daylight for hours and hours until our plane dropped gently down over the heads of cows and onto the Shannon Estuary, where it glided into Shannon Airport.

The airport was smaller than South Station in Boston and the air softer than any we had breathed before. We spent a night in a hotel near Shannon where there was a wedding going on all night and the words "Oh how we danced on the night we were wed" played over and over in some distant room. Then we were herded into a bus and headed for Dublin where the clouds were much lower than they were in America. My sister and I gulped in the atmosphere of a new country; it entered our systems like a potion that suffuses the whole and would never leave either of us. It was our mother's body.

In her novel *Mount Venus,* she wrote of the kind of room we occupied at her old home in Dublin: "The floor was uneven, with a slight list to starboard. It was bare except for one or two Celtic mats, several rickety chairs and a studio couch covered with green rugs, and beside it a bookcase full of Anglo-Irish literature. Separated from the sitting-room by a wooden partition was a combination bath and kitchenette. The nearness of the gas stove to the toilet made fulfillment of the bodily functions extremely precarious, especially as there was always a kettle on the boil. The walls were hung with Irish landscapes, good, bad, and indifferent."

Meanwhile back in Harvard Yard experts were drawing up shapes for the countries of the world. As Melville said about the invisibility that lies before us, it ensured that the future was being formed in fright. The mushroom cloud loomed as only past and future can, when they are united by a single image.

⚘

We returned home at the end of the summer and soon after moved to a whole house on a hilly street off Brattle Street in Cambridge. In 1949 my mother gave birth to a third daughter, Helen, and began to work at creating a small theater devoted to the spoken word (the Poets Theater); and finally we grew to know our father under the oppressive atmosphere of the cold war. We also tuned in to the unhappiness and incompatibility of our parents. We now had access to books of war photographs that showed the soldiers fallen, the buildings fallen, and the starving residents of Auschwitz against the wires.

It was 1950 when F. O. Matthiessen committed suicide by throwing himself out of a twelfth-story hotel window in Boston. Was it out of fear because he had participated in fellow-traveling committees and had signed left-wing petitions, had supported Trotskyist labor leader Ray Dunne? Or was it because he was homosexual and dreaded exposure? In any case, with devastating precision, Harry Levin at Harvard called his suicide "a dramatic refusal to enter the 2nd half of the twentieth century."

This act was received as a devastating public statement about the ability of one intellectual to survive the postwar years. It was also prophetic. The struggle to foster a culture informed by art and literature was soon to be stifled by the military, scientific, and monetary complex. Some people knew this and found the loss unbearable; most didn't notice.

⅄

In her first novel after leaving Ireland my mother wrote of one of her characters: "He leaned on the rail and looked down into the green waters, and the sea gulls screaming around the ship echoed the sadness in his own heart. The Ireland he had known was dead and gone, and in its place he felt something alien and vaguely menacing. So much had happened since he had last stood on that deck watching for the line of the Wicklow Hills to loom along the horizon. . . . He loved the look of it: green grass growing down to grey rocks, white cottages streeling up the mountain-sides, the ever-changing clouds, and the long, low line of hills—and the spire of Kingstown church a thin black line against the pearly sky."

She was perpetually homesick for Dublin, her mother, her brother and sister, and friends there. Yet the Dublin where she had spent her childhood (1905–25) was gone forever. Only the taste of alcohol, gooseberry jam on brown bread, and Irish butter and the red and blue curtsies of fuchsia would perform the amanuensis.

✸

In one of her notebooks a young French woman (Simone Weil) wrote, "One must believe in the reality of time. Otherwise one is just dreaming. For years I have recognized this flaw in myself, the importance it represents, and yet I have done nothing to get rid of it. What excuse could I be able to offer? Hasn't it increased in me since the age of ten?"

To resist the reality of time is to resist leaving childhood behind. She called this resistance a flaw in herself, but is it? The self is not the soul, and it is the soul (coherence) that lives for nine years on earth in a potential state of liberty and harmony. Its openness to metamorphosis is usually sealed up during those early years until the self replaces the soul as the fist of survival.

She refused to buy the world on the terms it was offered to her (hammer of time, measure of value) because of the effects of a single childhood relationship. As a child, she struggled to survive losing to her brother and his phenomenal brain; and after the age of nine she began to construct an alternate set of conditions.

A few photos show her with him. He was three years older. They stood together dressed in white; he was wearing a sailor suit;

they stood hand in hand, belly to belly, looking at the camera in 1911; then in another snapshot he sat in a little chair with his sandaled feet crossed while she leaned her head next to his. In 1916 they stood on a path with their legs uneven, she still leaned toward him and was dressed in white. And in 1922 they were seated at a table under some pine trees with books and big smiles. Here he was no longer a child and they look close in age. This was around the time she considered suicide, having realized that she could never achieve the learned heights of her brother, a scientific genius.

I see shadows when I remember these photos and white light dissolving on a path. She lives in the shadow of her brother, but she wears a crooked and charming expression for the camera. She is like someone who moves her body instead of the umbrella in order to get free of the rain and sun. From some accounts we have we learn that her brother struck her at times for her stupidity and then guiltily ordered her to strike him back. She obeyed and the striking sometimes turned into a fight until the parents intervened.

Like other siblings they read fairy tales together and learned how fixed a person's character is. Fate's kitchen is where the ingredients are dealt out. Temperament, body, social structure—these would determine a whole set of future events and choices. A person performs a good or evil act only because she was fated to do so. The grotesque folk tales that revealed the potential of the civilized world to bake people in ovens and poison them with charm were just around the corner.

There were other stories too. Hafiz the poet wrote lines that would have pleased her as a child: "One day the sun admitted, I am just a shadow. I wish I could show you the infinite incandescence that has cast my brilliant image. I wish I could show you (when you are lonely or in darkness) the astonishing light of your own being."

Her brother became increasingly skeptical with the cocky assurance of the scientist he would become. Surely his point of view would prevail, impervious to doubt, in the mainstream of scientific imperialism.

His sister tried something else to control her inferiority. She made it into a good thing! She lost even more, but now deliberately. She chose the least-valued object between them; she made sure neither had more than the other unless it was he who had more. She found it unpleasant when her parents scolded him for something mean he did to her. She could not stand any acts of preference or the sight of someone being punished. This way she broke down the conventional posture of her self in relation to other selves, and preserved the transcendence of childhood instead.

As the years went by, and as many know, her brother became increasingly valued as a mathematician. He was a remote professor who, when asked, said of his sister and himself, "We saw each other only rarely, speaking to one another most often in a humorous vein." When editing her notebooks for publication, he removed her pages of mathematical equations that she had carefully scrawled there, because he was ashamed of her errors.

There is a strange power of resistance that takes hold of certain weak and incompetent people. They refuse to give up, despite a series of blows, errors, and disappointments.

They annoy well-adjusted people because weakness is not meant to survive. There are many stories about weak children in folk and fairy tales and anyone can see that even if one of them has failed in the world, she has power radiating from her interior life.

⚼

Like most children I made no choices, but was battered about and landed by chance into the areas I admired. As I drifted through the dreary hours in school, I did poorly in everything but learning languages. French and Latin came to me easily. On the whole I felt like a nonentity who existed only as a flash, and to this day I am surprised when someone says *Hello, Fanny.*

A persistent questioning went along with this. What was it I knew already? What was the solid vessel filled with information that was the body itself? It was just a matter of discovering where the sounds were: inside or outside or somewhere between; upstairs, downstairs, or in my mother's chamber. The sound of a French poem punctuated by rhyme was the sound of a river, interrupted by waves and peaks, but still traveling as one thing.

I knew that I knew much that I didn't know that I knew. So I was a re-reader who rarely read new books. My first independent interest began with an anthology of poems from around the world with photographs in back of each poet's portrait, bust, or real face. I was drawn to the cold and even tone of certain translations. Arthur Waley's translations from the Chinese (like this poem "The Cranes" by Po Chü-i) hit the same pitch, tone, and cadence as early Celtic poetry.

> The western wind has blown but a few days;
> Yet the first leaf already flies from the bough.

On the drying paths I walk in my thin shoes;
In the first cold I have donned my quilted coat.
Through shallow ditches the floods are clearing away;
Through sparse bamboos trickles a slanting light.
In the early dusk, down an alley of green moss,
The garden-boy is leading the cranes home.

In this translation from the Chinese language is a new and strange language: a little lost as if ripped loose from anchor. In such linguistic distance, I found beauty; but a lonely echo, too, like an echo from the war that was fought overseas.

There would be no way I could remove the presence of that imagined violence from my first impressions of the world. In this sense I was one with multitudes of children who have started their lives in the shadow of a near or faraway war, one that caused permanent mental disturbance through the hysterical airwaves and removed a parent from their lives for a significant period of time.

꽃

I cannot measure how deep the shadows went in our household, but they translated into noise. My mother's impassioned shouts, my sister's echoing enthusiasm. My father's silent unhappiness, and him squeezed in his study, one light on, working. My mother upstairs in her room, when she wasn't at work, was emotionally overloaded and often in a delirium fueled by vodka. For decades my mother pretended my sister Susan was the child of another, an Irish man whom she liked better than my father, but none of us knew if either man was ever aware of this. The two men looked so alike, one being a taller version of the other, the fantasy could be fueled until DNA settled it.

It was the fifties and the House Un-American Activities Committee was in full swell when she found her American cause. It allowed her to transport elements of her early experience to America. In 1950 my mother founded the Poets Theater in Cambridge with a group of friends. Yeats's plays were performed and her adaptation from *Finnegans Wake* even traveled out of the Boston area, with Tom Clancy of the soon to be Clancy Brothers playing the lead. Irish actors slept in our basement and attic and wandered the house between. Before we went to Ireland, that soft cloudy land had been absorbed into the war experience for us children; it was rain-green in a sea of gray newsprint and explosives. Ever since our trip in 1947, the sound of an Irish voice was steeped with significance, innuendo, music.

The Poets Theater rehearsals took place in our house. My father hid away in his study. From the street someone walking by could have thought he was overhearing dysfunctional family dramas, shouts, weeping, soliloquies of outrage and despair. My mother generally did not need her quota of vodka on these active nights and was in full command of her directorial abilities. But between intoxication and drama, each night was a monster's ball at home.

My sister Susan had made a hit in Archibald MacLeish's play *The Trojan Horse* and acted in the Poets Theater plays from time to time. She was famous for her lovely sculpted face and her gifts as an actress. It was our father she resembled, his strong cheekbones, his deep-set eyes, his ears, his resistance to food, his scholarliness, his nervousness; but it was with my mother that she was closely allied in her inclinations and interests.

The stairs at home became the household dividing line for me, imaginatively and psychologically. When I think of my early childhood, I rarely see the inside of a room, but only the stair-case with the door open to our parents' room at the top, a mirror on the right and the banister that I climbed up and over and slid along and the stairs where I sat and stared either up or down. I let people pass by, exaggeratedly moving out of the way. The stairs were my territory that I occupied on my way to somewhere up or down; and as I look back I see this positioning as typical of the vacillation that would become my fatal flaw.

For after all, whose child was I? My mother of the Poets Theater or my father of social conscience? They were irreconcilably different in nature and commitment. The original choice for children, before racial and national and even gender identities have been raised, is the choice of parent. Which one am I genetically fated to follow? Which one will I choose to follow? Who is my favorite? Whose favorite am I?

There I would sit, halfway up the stairs, listening to rehearsals with my mouth open and my eye on my father's study lamp glowing through his doors. My fear of performance had its origins here. I preferred my father and his political conversations, but the activity and pleasure that trailed the poets around our house were irresistible. I had my mother's weaknesses for having fun and wasting time. But something in me, invisible and constrained, belonged entirely to my father.

There was one night when I was forced to act with Lyon Phelps; we were the only two onstage, and the review the next morning said, "Fanny Howe played the part of a child and acted like one." Meantime in another theater my sister played Iphigenia, who was also a child but one my sister knew how to "play." She knew the difference between living and acting. She was trained by our mother to speak her lines and move gracefully. I was silly, giggling, and disobedient.

If anyone ever bossed me around, I was out the door; and any public appearance terrified me. It was as if my own existence, when acknowledged by an adult, was abhorrent to me. My suspicion of all grown-ups lasted for most of my adolescence and so there is no way I can report objectively on my mother's world. I was determined to close the entrance to the womb as fast as I could.

At the same time she had a physical potency that made me want to make her happy; I loved her if only because she let me cut school a lot. The singer Liam Clancy described her like this: "She had a presence. There was an aura of glee about her. Her eyes were full of life and devilment. Her face was a tangle of laugh lines that told of a lifetime of seeing delight and humor in the world around her. Her voice had a soft but compelling Anglo-Irish music to it."

The Poets Theater stood at 24 Palmer Street in Cambridge behind the Harvard Coop. You climbed a narrow flight of stairs and on the right was the reception room where people gathered before the play and during intermissions; and straight ahead was the room that seated sixty with a couple of rows precariously placed on wooden planks at the back. There was a table for tickets to the left as you entered. There were all the bulbs and bars for the lighting overhead, a curtained backdrop, and often a stage set designed by an artist and lit by a student. Backstage did not offer much space for crouched actors waiting for their cues, so they galloped up and down the stairs into the smell of paste and face cream.

Down on Palmer Street and to the left of number 24 was Morris Pancoast's antique shop where all the costumes were kept and many mirrors; he huddled in the back, white, bald, small, old, pointed, bemused, uncritical, watching the changing of the clothes and the application of makeup. The actors had to speed through the freezing cold and rain to gallop up the fire escape and dash backstage to await their turns. V. R. (Bunny) Lang was secretary for the theater in a big fur coat, bleached blond hair, and sexy red lips, and Richard Eberhart and Lyon Phelps (long and thin, dry and sad) were her bosses. The first play was *Try! Try!* by Frank O'Hara and was designed by Edward Gorey (long, morose, ironic, and damp). No one asked what good was poetry in such a brutal world. The Poets Theater dedicated itself to the resonance of language as a counterpoint to a theater of intention.

My mother involved herself at once by using her experience in Dublin, where various readings and performances took place in people's houses before moving onto the stage. So around the big houses of Cambridge, carloads of young actors would arrive with scripts to entertain professors, their wives, and anyone in the art world who wanted to come and listen to a play reading. They took it seriously, though to an outsider it was weird, useless, and all in vain. Drinks, of course, were served.

It would be very hard to describe how it all survived without a sponsor or a five-year plan because every day was a crisis day there; money was always lacking, audiences were last minute, and the drama was only onstage briefly. The performed play seemed to be an outcome of daily failures made up of panics and hysterical patchwork rehearsals, hurried choices for plays, quarrels, and a constant turnover of students for help with sets, lights, costumes, props. And there were many, many plays performed. They were new; they were Irish, European, or American; they were short, long, poetic, prosaic, historical, contemporary political; and by young, old, unknown, and known writers alike.

My mother and her cofounders (Lyon Phelps, Bunny Lang, Felicia Lamport, Edward Gorey) chose the most unconventional dramas they could unearth for the Cambridge crowd. *The Bald Soprano* by Ionesco; verse plays by Ashbery, O'Hara, Merwin, Gorey, Paul Goodman, Donald Hall, and Anne Sexton; and Richard Wilbur's *The Misanthrope* were premiered on that stage, as was my mother's adaptation of *Finnegans Wake*.

Like Ken Russell's *The Devils,* many of the productions were dedicated to camp and excess. *The Devils* is a "true" story about the possession of nuns by devils in seventeenth-century Loudun, France. Sacrificed to their sexual hysteria and dementia is an innocent if sexy priest named Urbain Grandier. The Poets Theater was hysterical and raised the question that can become a psychosis: Are people what they seem to be or is the human phenomenon a fake? When I saw the Ken Russell movie years later, I realized that of course the people are not so much artificial as they are devils all the way through.

☀

If the point of God is that "God knows" when no one else does, then the point of a parent might be the same. In the case of a parent who lives in the gaslight district of her imagination, the gas is either going up or going down because something is going on in another room, not in the one where the child is wildly attempting to win her approval. My mother entertained herself by forcing my sister and me to compete for her attention. But it was a double bind. In this act there was no winning because the first had already been chosen. (In years to come, my sister Susan would become a scholar and poet, and my sister Helen would choose an outdoor, muscular, and sculptor's life over the indoor one we had been raised in.)

One Sunday afternoon, in the late fifties, a black tunnel of smoke spilled across Cambridge. My parents, my sister Helen, and I stood outside watching and wondering what it was. It was the Poets Theater burning to the ground, with tapes and scripts included in the conflagration. All gone to char. It was the end of an era, and I remember that my mother, used to such endings, was remarkably serene about it.

❅

I have a recurrent dream, have had it for decades; it is so familiar that I can steer my way through it, wondering if I will see the same corner again and the same apartment, visit the same people and wind up in streets behind Harlem, way, way up, narrow streets, drains, crusts, symptoms of old wounds. It was another home, another family, my real one there, that I came from. I am happy to be back but always fear I will not find the train station, or if I do, it will take me in a direction away from home. The water in the Harlem River is murky and yet it leads to a lovely green promontory and more green beyond. I am standing there again, and again. The water and the spits of sandbars swabbed in green grass are the outcome of Harlem, not the remnants of a world before Harlem. The dreams of the people had oozed out onto the river. I head down, with this vision on my right, and on my left there is the scablike city, friends behind windows and walls, my friends and a family of the dream. This dream tells me that I lived here before. Otherwise, why would I have no fear and know when to take the turn that drives down into the wide square?

❅

Now the flowering sun is yellow.
I have told the children about the dream. They listen, looking elsewhere.
They are brave children.

We are inside a little seaside café at Omaha Beach, where an existentialist smokes and sips from a tumbler of red wine. He owns the café.

He tells us what we can have: ice cream, tea, coffee, or wine.

I have tea but the children and Saskia have big ice cream bars.

Paul has coffee and my daughter smokes with the owner.

It is snowing outside the café. It falls on the waves and foam and on the cars and leaves. It looks the way music arrives in the brain and lights up a different cell until the brain is flooded with its sound or its silence.

Can dreams support the whole weight of the material world?

☀

Once a child stared out a schoolroom window into the sky shining between the leaves. They had deepened with the arrival of fall. Outside birds sang, music played in a distant room, cars squealed around a corner. The air lay against the glass pane like a cold hand.

The class is French, but the teacher is American, both soft of voice and face, a little wistful. Now the child hears a fire engine racing to a fire. She wonders if it is going to her house. It is certainly going in that direction, she hears as it veers around streets, and the siren weeps.

Now the teacher is taking out the textbook and so are all the children. The child at the window who is naturally gifted at languages and nothing else—they all agree—is invited to read some lines from a poem by Paul Verlaine: *"Il pleure dans mon coeur / comme il pleut dans la ville . . . "*

The teacher praises her for her French. It is the high point of her day.

The sky outside the window is wash-gray.
The teacher reads aloud: *"Mon coeur, comme un oiseau, volt-igeait tout joyeux . . . "*

The sound of the line is summer gone: in its lilt the cry (*coeur,* choir) of whip-poor-wills, cardinals, sparrows, seagulls, and geese that clamored as they sped (joy-voltage) through the sky over-head, necks extended, as if they breathed their honking. The sum-mer past: a shingled house and bent screens, the hours of liberty. Hours of reading: illustrations, in black and white pen, and gray wash, of animals and characters. The large pressed words on the yellowish paper. She listened extra-acutely in summer as the sun thinned: her mother's voice slurring, a shift toward slop, slight tone changes, a bitter flammable breath. The siren reminds her of practice air raids during the war, of the radio voices with those whines in the background, movies she has seen.

The influences came in a rush, together. But she felt that foreign words always came from the past. So they came first. They pre-ceded English rising from before, like a song floating through a windowpane with an unknown source. Foreign words seemed to drag hairy seaweeds and green slime, chipped edges and glossy forms along with them.
It was like standing in the sea and saying it was beautiful even as monstrous and unknown life twirled within it and brushed against her legs.
Le navire roulait sous un ciel sans nouages . . .
English (growing everywhere like grass) was unstable, stutter-ing, and wildly associative.
But the words did seem to aspire to one thing only: an aura larger than the limit and substance of their letters.

Who knows how and when she heard that line as a surrealist might: but she loved the French surrealist poets later on.

"The navy ruled Susan without clouds . . . "
"A ceiling was a solid rolling cloud . . . "
"The vessel unrolled a sky for the new ages . . . "
She loved to translate from the Latin too. The same teacher again there did not make anyone read Latin out loud, so she was saved from that embarrassment, but she would have to speak her translation into English.

Which came first—the look of the letter or the sound of the phrase? Who thought of those conjunctions of sound and object and appearance?

Way down the street the organ grinder played every day at the same time. His music signified being at home and not in school. Its cranky joy was inseparable from the joy of being safe away from teachers. The siren was going in the direction of her home.

She changed tenses.
She had always been a school-hating child. It was an affliction. Every weekday was formed in the hell of subordination. But her ears freed her and her eyes fixed on the shuffling branches. Gladly, she translated one sound into another. She bent a word, a noise, an image around and around in many versions. She listened to and looked at the Latin.

She memorized the French. *(If it is foreign to me, I am foreign to it.)*

Le bateau ivre . . .

The Drunken Boat. The boat is drunk!

The sea under the boat is drunk.

Drunk sea, rocking boat. On its way where, that bateau adult, that beastly woman, battling the ivy-green waves, drunk and evil?

The siren stopped at her house but nothing was on fire.

※

I wanted to leave everywhere from about the age of nine. This involved delinquency at school and withdrawal from the home scene. I didn't like grown-ups with the exception of my father and felt uncomfortable with what was given to me as a birthright and what later came to be understood (by me and my culture) as meaning: white.

White meant adult, condescending, cold, pale, driven, individualist, judging, and theoretical. White meant distant, detached, ironic, skeptical, and ambitious, Protestant.

My father was white but not quite. In 1952 Senator William E. Jenner of Indiana (and head of the Communist-hunting Jenner Committee) called three Harvard professors "Pink Boys and Campus Theorists." "Why they hate America so much, I don't know," said Jenner and named Arthur M. Schlesinger Sr., Francis Higgenson, and Mark Howe as the three pink boys. Soon after this a faculty member in the Harvard Medical School refused to testify about alleged Communist activities before the Senate's Jenner Committee. Dr. Helen Deane Markham and her husband were named as members of the Communist Party in 1947. She denied this and my father became involved in her legal defense. Meantime Harvard fired her, then (embarrassed) reappointed her—but only for the last few months of her term, when they made her leave permanently. Two other Harvard professors whom my father also defended legally—Wendell Furry (physics) and Leon Kamin, a research assistant in social relations—refused to name names to McCarthy but boldly gave him the dates of their own involvement in the party.

What McCarthy would do became a question of what Harvard would do, and then what my father and some of his friends would do. In this case, unlike the Markham one, Harvard did not dismiss the professors (called by McCarthy "Fifth Amendment

Communists"), and various colleagues fussed that Furry and Kamin were being stubborn in their own defense and should just clear out. But Harvard resisted firing them, having been called by McCarthy "the Kremlin on the Charles."

What I remember of all this is the door through which the FBI undercover agents came one night, and the way my father politely led them in and out of his bookish study. I remember the gaiety of the Poets Theater rehearsing in the living room with my mother, and my small, upright father shuttling the men out the door. The hall was dark and heaped with coats. The smell of a dinner cooked and eaten still hung on the stairs that led up to our bedrooms. (Years later FBI agents would come into my own house in Jamaica Plain and sit on a sofa with walkie-talkies in their pockets cross-examining me about members of my then family. It seemed inevitable that this would happen again.)

Every night in his study, my father sat correcting student papers and preparing lectures. At work, he wrote his letters to several senators, repeating his position that McCarthy was a far greater danger to the country than the people he was accusing of being Communists. The contempt that McCarthy and his Senate committees had for law was a way of "overthrowing the government," so what was democracy good for, if no one seemed to perceive this paradox and take action?

I asked him questions and always got answers touched with ambiguity. But plot can only be understood retroactively, and by the time a story is understood, most of the questions that were important earlier have been folded over into bewilderment. Still, there was one question that stayed fresh to him throughout my father's life. Which is more valuable to protect—liberty or equality? Are they, in fact, compatible?

The war and then the cold war were two major soul-forging events for him privately in that he applied his knowledge of law and the Constitution to difficult human dilemmas and in this way developed a perspective on the world similar to but not the same as that of his writing subject, Oliver Wendell Holmes.

His increasingly desolate view of existence as something without an ultimate cause or goal helped him in his work, since human nature showed no signs of improvement despite the warnings of the law or in the churches. He saw contradiction in power and depth in the poor and couldn't stand religiosity. He even remarked that perhaps atheists needed the protection of the law more than religions did, given the attacks on Communists as atheists, the upsurge in religious fundamentalism, and the casual dismissal of the First Amendment.

My father patiently tried to explain the Constitution and civil liberties to me and I became his sidekick in various campaign activities (local and presidential), and over the years we argued about certain national events, but usually I deferred to his erudition and sanity. I had thought that the great victory over McCarthyism meant that certain truths had been established: freedom of speech, freedom of association, and equal protection under the law. I thought that was the end of that problem. He disabused me of this notion in his next political action.

His involvement in the civil rights movement, the third great all-consuming interest of his life, after the war and McCarthy, galvanized all that he had learned through the first two. He might as well have put on his uniform and picked up his briefcase to enter a battlefield again. He taught and acted as a legal consultant, went south, and worked in the north on the busing issue. The spirit of the Constitution was, he believed, transparent. But race and religion were two recurrent dilemmas in the nation for a reason; they could be used to bring down the revolutionary nature of that spirit. Now I know that those who will restore the country's heart and direction will be those who have benefited least from the years since 1968.

My father worked for social justice and was eviscerated. I think when he died he had had enough. (Heart attacks can be a kind of suicide.) He just missed living to see the assassinations of Martin Luther King Jr. and Bobby Kennedy or watch how the separation of church and state, which was supposed to be a given and the equality of black Americans with white ones, beginning with education, were both set way back. Luckily he wasn't there when the Constitution was sold out and the Supreme Court became politicized to a degree never before imagined. The jails filled up and capital punishment increased. The Vietnam War ended but soon it was replaced with an even more profane, intentional war. He had supported my generation's commitment to progress and would been appalled at how it came to be seen as delusional. He died with the civil rights movement, and many of the causes that he worked for have been reversed or erased over the four decades following. For me his absence opened a door into a future as vertiginous as a long fall.

☀

I see the snow has slowed now and random idle flakes float, the way the words about them might (piece by piece) in a story by Hans Christian Andersen. The grave city of Boston is at a distance from where I sit. Still, it is home. My father is buried at Quincy graveyard. He died in 1967 after a meeting on school busing in Roxbury, and shoveling snow. It was the end of safety for me. After that there would be more assassinations and less grounded action except in Vietnam. And then the light would change and the orientation of energy and possibility would radically alter.

In the 1960s I didn't take drugs or listen to the Rolling Stones. I drank cheap wine and listened to folk music and Motown. Like most everyone I knew, I was penniless, incompetent, and unable to decipher the signs of the adult world. The violence of wars around the world had seeped into the collective mind, causing a blur of reactions. But when my father died, it was as if the strange fears of childhood were at last being realized. It was the imagined loss coming to fruition twenty years later after that war was over and he had long since come home from it.

Violence, as it says in the Zohar, causes actual disturbance in the heavens as it does in the upper spheres of the human imagination. The despair of a father does the same. It is the same as the subtle social nihilism that is manifested as pragmatism. Nihilism will build the contraptions it lacked and butcher animals; it will persevere in generating myths and hierarchies; it will seduce children and torture for erotic delight. It will despise the kind of weakness that survives by changing form. As Nietzsche said, "Nihilism is . . . not only the belief that everything deserves to perish; but one actually puts one's shoulder to the plough; *one destroys.*"

Why did he talk so much to me about suicide? Was this prophetic? Suicide is "any action which is done with the idea in mind that it will lead to death." It can be done as a matter of conscience, for honor's sake, in a state of selfless devotion to a cause, in despair, and as a way to avoid doing something that harms others. But maybe the word is not despair in fact, but something closer to the word used by Baudelaire:

It's BOREDOM. Tears have glued its eyes together.
You know it well, my Reader. This obscene
beast chain-smokes yawning for the guillotine . . .

❦

The quest for a condition that exists in two separate states is what confuses people like me. The person looking for a fixed identity is often the same person looking for God (escape into emptiness). This split search can only be folded into one in the process of working on something—whether it is building, digging, accounting, painting, teaching—with a wholeheartedness that qualifies as complete attention. In such a state you find yourself depending on an unknown model to supply you with the focus to complete what you are doing. Your work is practical, but your relationship is always potential in the range of its errors and failures. You align yourself with some ethereal figure behind and ahead and above you; you call on it for help, realizing the vacillation and inadequacy of your acts, your words.

❦

The formation of our relationship to the world (for some of us) is experienced as an unfolding; it imitates the material cycle of larva, pupa, cocoon. It begins as if at the egg, blind and bound, and in its infancy it discovers light and a trail. The light is everywhere but apportioned as if it were an extra endowment. The coming trail is often determined by the birth home where each parent glides in a dance of oppositions before the new creature who is entranced and confused.

The creature must shuck, melt, and bend those figures into malleable functions if it is to break out of its buglike condition and head for the light. If it can retain all its cycles as layers of knowing that can be accessed throughout its life and not crush or dry them up one by one, it will live in the green of the natural world. It will be what is called a free spirit. Otherwise, it will only survive as a self locked into the dense furniture of sense and tradition, like one blinded by fear.

Paradoxically, no matter how strong our parents are, we have to knock them off in order to carry the body of our childhood safely through the world. Our childhood's body will be composed of those two. Which one is our legitimate parent, the one we claim we belong to, only our psyche knows. A person won't have the answers until she has slipped out into the larger world, without either of them anywhere.

⁂

I fell in love with Liam Clancy when I was a teen and he was acting and singing for the Poets Theater. He wrote a song for the *Countess Cathleen* that he sang in his mild but roaming Irish voice. He was three years older and poised for immense success in New York without having any foreknowledge of that. Women already were circling around him, sensing his gift and his amiability. After-school hours we spent with his guitar and reciting poetry on the banks of the Charles River, trips to Greenwich Village, wanderings at night through the lilac-bent streets of Cambridge, endless talking and kissing on the front porch of my house. No other later romance would hold for me such mutual devotion, poetry, chastity, and tenderness. It all came back to me in one novel I wrote years later but now transformed into a steed of exaggerated recollection. Still, there is little as liberating as the discovery that you have the same memory of a single event as someone you loved years before.

"For a moment I felt I was in Dublin," Liam wrote in his recent memoir. "It was the coloring you see so often there, with the lights reflected on the Liffey from the far bank. . . . I crawled over and sat beside Fanny, and a lovely feeling of peace fell upon my soul. The heat, the light, the sky, the warmth of love, life felt beautiful. I lay back and Fan lay back with her head on my arm and we made pictures in the clouds."

☀

Here is a little poem by Priscian, the Irish monk who stayed in Switzerland in the ninth century:

A wall of forest looms above
  and sweetly the blackbird sings;
all the birds make melody
  over me and my books and things.

There sings to me the cuckoo
  from bush-citadel in grey hood.
God's doom! May the Lord protect me
  Writing well, under the great wood.

God's doom! Fear is everywhere and suddenly erupts. There is no containing it, not even from a poem by a contented monk.

☀

One winter day the children and I walked down the avenue de la Gare.
We crossed the place de la Résistance and ended up on the avenue of the 6th of June.

Then we took the train to Bayeux in a blizzard, talking about war.

The children would later toss chunks of snow over the stone railing into the neat black river.

A skeleton had recently been discovered in the marshes beyond Utah Beach and ice storms had moved from Northern Ireland clear across England and France.

Winds would follow tomorrow.

The weather people admitted they could only really predict three days ahead and then they entered into the zone of probability and unknown influence.

A lamppost trembled in the wind and a newspaper blew by, reporting on more suicide blasts the day before.

That day the news would always be old and our knowing too late.

Things we had already witnessed the night before:

Three bad boys stuffed toilet paper down the girls' toilet in a KFC in Portsmouth and one of them got slapped in the face by a stranger for it. He cried out, "He GBF'd me." He was about nine and already knew the term "gross bodily force."

Chicken skin was stuck to the linoleum beside his feet.

We slept like vagabonds on the ship's floor and a white man glared at us because the children and their mother were not white. You can spot that look.

Still the trip was poetic.

Later a poet accused us of being saints because we were happy in adversity.

The children's faces grew red with the flames. They couldn't drink the soup and the youngest sat on a stool.

Paul ate all his food.

We had gone from one brasserie to the next looking for children's meals. An Englishman who was a voluntary military scholar told us that "D" stands for "Day" in "D-Day."

"My father was a colonel in the North African campaign," I told him and the children watched his face for a reaction.

There is a ballooning stiffness, a stitch in my chest, as if my heart would burst, no pain, when I lean a certain way to tie my shoelaces and tell the children a joke at the same time.

Paul said only God should fly at thirty-five thousand feet.

We were all foreigners for those days.

Where the experience of translation outlasted the theory of it.

Borders become clusters of confusion when there is a good-bye. Even the uninvolved passersby, the cars, birds, and wind are momentarily disturbed and seem to falter, and switch direction.

Dogs pause and look around.

A good-bye generates a moment of chaos in the immediate environment: those saying good-bye sense the trap in which they are forever held, the jet of light that produces their flesh for that second, and the fact that there is no backward or forward in time.

Be safe—you don't want to say these words to children.

Instead I reminded them that Br'er Rabbit knew how to extract himself from the tar and brambles, so he could afford to get stuck to them.

America

We know one thing. Poverty has to exist for capitalism to continue. As long as the cash flow is preserved within an outer circle of raw destitution, the country is safe from social welfare.

If there were no outer circle of swamp and procreation, populations without dental records or medical documents or photo IDs, there would have to be a welfare state with health care and housing provided to all. There would have to be an evening out, all the way to the edge.

As long as the culture of poverty is maintained as a perpetual problem, the benefits of being healthy and comfortable are inarguable and must be paid for.

All those beds, clothes, threads lumpish and loose from water and weight, all those mobile homes, the weeping, more water to cope with, the bowels, more sewage, pets lost and grandparents swept away, more mosquitoes, more bites to make more illness. Meds for psychosis, diabetes, AIDS, and depression—soaked and missing.

Outside and inside bodies washed around in the waters of their neighborhoods, the rooftop people called for help, or there were the holdouts who sipped their coffee while the wind raged, muttering, "I'm not moving."

The light hides in the top yellow leaves and at the tips of buildings and the cold air just at knee level. This is what it was like when the planes flew over Manhattan, the sky was an abnormal cerulean blue.

Today a woman in New Orleans thanked Jesus when she was handed a drink of water. We saw her on television.

Why did the woman thank Jesus instead of the man who brought it to her?

I mean, if she thinks Jesus brought the glass of water, who brought the flood that made her thirsty?

Tell me, why did the woman thank Jesus?

What if you were to tell her that not only did Jesus die two thousand years ago, but he did not come back and does not exist in any possible sense today.

What if you were to tell her that she should thank the man in front of her instead and ask him his name.

What if you were to tell her that we stand alone on a planet and when she is given a glass of water, it follows from a series of causes that have made it an inevitable gesture.

And so she should thank the man, not Jesus, for the water since he was the faithful member of a chain of neighborly acts.

Or maybe this is what she meant.

Person, Place, and Time

1.

In 1958 I was shipped off to Paris having failed to get into any college, unlike my friends at school. My father needed to find me somewhere to go. My only strength was French. So I was sent to continue to learn French at a school in Sèvres. But I jumped over the wall one night and fled the school and made my way into Paris, where I had a good time with my mother's childhood and lifelong friend Samuel Beckett from Dublin, who took me around with him for a few days. He was tall, solicitous, and bemused as he took me through parks and in and out of cafés where he was once stopped by a young admirer but otherwise had the status of an ordinary man to both strangers and me. I noted down what he said in my diary because he did seem to know things. I must have asked him where is a good place for a writer to write, because he answered, "In the fireplace," referring to Descartes. We went to see *The Cranes Are Flying* with his companion, who never said a word because she only spoke French. We visited their apartment, and then finally my father figured out what to do with me.

I was called home to prepare for college. He had pulled strings and had gotten me into Stanford at the last minute. It was a time when they wanted people from the East Coast. So west I went, ever eager to travel far from home and to suffer from homesickness at the same time.

Stanford was far from being a center for beatnik or radical activity, though it was susceptible to their influence. Without much difficulty I found friends with politics like my own and moved in a circle of young Marxists with guitars and motorcycles and went to San Francisco whenever possible.

Two of my great academic experiences were taking a course on *Moby Dick* from Yvor Winters and hearing Frank O'Connor lecture on the short stories of Coppard, Chekhov, and other Russians. He had a theory for these stories that he called "the lonely voice" and that he passionately supported with his lectures. I took a fiction workshop with Malcolm Cowley, who turned off his earphone and dozed during most of class. He concluded his year at Stanford with a public address in which he stated that no great American writer would come out of a fiction workshop.

I majored in European history, read all I could on the Russian Revolution, still believing in its original ideals. (As a child I had made a clay bust of Stalin to present to my grieving mother on the day he died.) Outside class I spent my time getting washed down the steps of city hall protesting capital punishment and attending blacklisting sessions in the courthouse, going to North Beach poetry readings, and dropping out of college. Northern California was fraught with political activities away from the Republican blonds who reigned over the Stanford campus.

The prevailing writers were all male: Kerouac, Kesey, Patchen, Rexroth, Spicer, Ginsberg, Ferlinghetti, and Corso. It was the same configuration I had seen since childhood: the women shuffling barefoot around the edges of masculine territory, or tossed onto pallets on the floor, long-haired, obedient, like the women in the movie about Chet Baker called *Let's Get Lost*. I wanted my father to know that I was, at last, his revolutionary sidekick and reported home to him regularly.

One sunny day my close friend was killed on the back of a friend's motorcycle and I dropped out of Stanford for the third time, eloping with an older man, a microbiologist from New York. We lived in Berkeley, where I wrote pulp fiction for money. It was this bitter pretend marriage that planted the seeds of my claustrophobia. I never returned to college and never got a degree.

And if I had never married this man, it would have been a brief, first sexual encounter. But I was interested in ending my virginity legally and I was under his spell. He looked like Christopher Plummer. He wined, dined, and dressed me. He taught me how to cook gourmet. Eggs Benedict and oranges filled with sherbet and capped with toasted meringue. He was a man without humor, but intelligence and wit, who had had a cold childhood. But he insisted that it was my fault and not his mother's who made him so cold. (See *A Gentle Woman* by Bresson.)

Reno marked the end of my first experience with California. Only in my collection of stories, *Forty Whacks,* did I reenter that period of my life.

⚘

You could say an event in history is over, the way a book is slapped shut when it is done. But where is the marker? Time and direction are both forces that work together to crush willpower. Time without direction could have no sequence or differentiation; time like the wind either allows or prevents actions. And without an action there would be no past, present, or future in any direction.

Why do we always think history is full of stops and starts? The future is only the past turned around to look at itself.

2.

In my midtwenties and divorced, I first saw the poet Robert Lowell when I was dining with my father at the Harvard Faculty Club. It was my father who pointed him out to me where he was seated alone at a table for two beside a cold dark window. Thoughtful and solitary, he looked the way I imagined a poet should. It was two years before I saw him again and only weeks after my father died. He was the first real poet I would come to know on my own terms and he arrived as a father figure, or a figment of my real father already imaginary.

Our conversations mostly revolved around "the problem with Boston," mutual friends, books, poets he admired (Ginsberg, Williams, Stevens, Rich) and ones I admired, and his bitter, pellucid narratives about history and current events, always punctuated with laughter. I never showed him my poems. Perhaps because of this, there was no disappointment associated with any moment of our friendship.

His poetry was the most famous in America at this time; his influence on the generation just under his was fixed. *Life Studies* and *Lord Weary's Castle* introduced confession and internal rhyme into free verse and showed how personal autobiography could be of interest to everyone. He was part of a new wave in translation, much of it from the Russian, and he wrote plays that were immediately performed. He wrote all the time, and soon this fever developed into notebooks of poems, poems that stayed close to him, reproducing in a single form, the sonnet, that could flow as easily and frequently as was possible.

Since that time Lowell's work has been diverted into a tide of imitations and most recently into a whole new school of thought about poetry. He is more securely placed in the current British canon than he is in the American. Poetry is like science that way; it has its day and use, and is absorbed into a process or discarded. Any poet knows that his or her work is just another part of nature and all the papers will return to rot, perhaps having left a little shadow on a brain somewhere, or in a collective culture. The hope is only that its interest will last the length of your child's or your student's lifetime, or it will be a part of your generation's story.

When I knew Lowell, he seemed indomitable, and one thought that he, like Wordsworth, would last even longer than anyone. His poems seemed radical and strong even to those, like me, who were following a different beat. At the time the poems of Lowell's that I read the most were his "imitations" of poems by poets who are not American.

These include adaptations of Baudelaire, Rimbaud, Mallarmé, Pasternak, Montale, Sappho, Leopardi because they prove that there is a simultaneity of thought among poets. The dominant idea of "influence" was always suspect to me, so these poems translated by Lowell fueled my belief in another process going on among poets. I saw this process as being horizontal and irrational. I still see it this way. There is a confluence of conditions that produces a movement among poets from the United States to China. We change together. And we change in a range of time that is like a great pond where we are born to swim in relation to each other as in Lowell's version of Baudelaire's *Correspondences*:

> Nature is a temple where the living pillars
> Sometimes emit confused speech;
> Man passes through the forests of symbols
> Which watch him with familiar gazes.
>
> As far off echoes from a distance meld
> In a shadowy and profound unity,
> Vast as the night and vast as the light,
> Perfumes, colors and sounds correspond.

This vision of correspondences was more credible to me than the theory of the unconscious and would, in fact, remain part of that vocation of mine that has no name.

Many years after Lowell died I scanned the whole text of his life in his poems and letters and realized I had only been reading fragments of a single note before. All together, it is an uninterrupted arc formed from the sound of poems. I think the past always looks most complete when no one is in it.

3.

Here the chronology becomes strangely chaotic, the parts smashed together and pressed and turned like lumps of wet clay. The years are inseparable and gray like the world of lost people, loved or unknown. For a while I reeked of paregoric, an across-the-counter brown liquid opiate that stills the guts. Always nervous, always afraid of being away from the sanctuary of the public restroom and home, of the terrible pains coming at the wrong time, this chronic affliction directed and undermined my daily activities from an early age. And now I was claustrophobic. I didn't tell people about any of it, but swallowed the paregoric and fought off the gathering and increasing waves of alienation that had been building out of some undiagnosed misery.

Was it an event, a prolonged condition, or a memory I couldn't remember?

In the blindness that gives us the necessity to move, I tapped my way from one city to another with an Olivetti typewriter and paper, no money, the notebooks of Camus, Jean Genet's novels, James Baldwin, and a longing for love that was as powerful as a physical illness. Divorced and disappointed too early, I was, for five years, as they used to say, loose.

I lived on the Bowery in poverty and abandon like most of my friends, working as a reader for Avon Books and writing novels and poems. I had places to go but it was for love I lived. But what was love? It was a quality I could not recognize. I confused it with sex, but also with its own absence. What love wasn't became what it was. An absence of kindness or generosity, warmth, or ease became the reminders of what love must be. Being in the presence, therefore, of a cold, neurotic, and unkind male was identical to existing in the memory of the opposite. I stared past him, reassembling. This was not masochism because there was no pleasure anywhere. It was anamnesis, or the reenactment of a love affair that I imagined or perhaps had when I was too young to recognize its quality. I was remembering by waiting for the past to return. The horizon was behind me or perhaps ahead. This is when I began to be conscious of another form of time, barely and blurrily, but one upon which I could muse.

Eric Emerson, of the Warhol films, spooned DMT into my coffee when I vowed I would never take drugs. I was only saved from permanent psychosis by a large dose of thorazine given to me by my roommate's shrink. After that I still never did take drugs, but I loved my wine and dancing at the Dom in silver lamé and sitting on the roof with my dog Woofer. I was a hatcheck girl at Joe Allen's in the theater district and read many great novels stuffed against wet coats in the corner of a cubby. All my lights went out when I couldn't pay the bill and stayed like that right through the big blackout in New York City.

During this interlude Frank MacShane, the biographer of Raymond Chandler, introduced me to the work of Edward Dahlberg. He gave me his book *Because I Was Flesh* and then, when I was finished, he gave me his address so I could write a fan letter. I had never done such a thing before. Dahlberg answered me immediately and for months I would receive letters from him that were both solicitous and patriarchal. In a certain sense these letters changed the course of my emotional thought.

Dahlberg who was said to be the originator of the proposition that one perception must immediately lead to the next—a proposition that drove American poetics from after the war on—was not a poet unless you call a highly charged, iambic, metaphorical prose "poetry." Some people call *Moby Dick* a poem. I call *Because I Was Flesh* a poem as well as Dahlberg's less-known book, *Bottom Dogs*. Perhaps it is simply a term of respect for those who push language to its limit.

Dahlberg left a burn mark on whomever he met; he branded his students and friends and then abandoned them as his mother had for a time abandoned him. He even broke off with the other priapic genius Charles Olson over the value of *Moby Dick*. Dahlberg wrote that *"Moby Dick* is gigantology, a tract about a gibbous whale and fifteen or more lawless seamen, who are alone, by choice, though they are together." He was against Melville, who may have been too close to being an influence rather than a companion.

He grew up in Missouri, the son of a lady barber. And in order to get a flavor of the man one must read lines like these, describing the orphanage where he spent childhood time:
"They were a separate race of stunted children who were clad in famine. Swollen heads lay on top of ashy uniformed orphans. Some had oval or oblong skulls; others gigantic watery occiputs described by Hesiod and Pliny. The palsied and the lame were cured in the pool of Bethesda, but who had enough human spittle to heal the orphans' sore eyes and granulated lids?"

Dahlberg talked and wrote like this. He and Olson met while at Harvard soon after the war. Dahlberg was ten years older and probably not as full of certitude as he became later. But he made his mark on that huge young Olson, who was then studying with F. O. Matthiessen in the American literary studies program. Olson's work would always return to postwar European philosophy and American politics and his theories on poetics grew out of these interests. The autodidactic Dahlberg, on the other hand, identified entirely with the proletarian underground since the twenties and with ancient texts. He went into seven years of withdrawal from writing to study these. His first book, *Bottom Dogs*, had an introduction by D. H. Lawrence. After his withdrawal, he renounced his former self, his politics, everyone he knew, almost everyone who aspired to write, and his own early works.

In a letter to me in December 1966 he wrote:

"Now, you can't admire Tolstoi along with Joyce, Jane Austen and Henry James. That's the usual academic pother of the day. Should you have understood Tolstoi you won't be able to read the famous rubbish of James, Joyce and Austen. You must learn how to expurge what is foolish, bad garbage; otherwise you'll never find those values you long for and should possess. Now, I know it is well-nigh impossible to give people good advice, particularly when you've got no doctrine or dogma to go along with it. But just take from an experienced worm of prose style that this kind of chaotic and amorphous thinking will be a fell obstacle to your own ripening."

We met in cafés in New York and once at Elaine's, where he was disgusted by the pleasures that he saw. I was proud to be with him, my secret teacher, and only Frank MacShane shared my interest, my desire to please him. He sent me a list of writers I was instructed to read by June 1967.
This is that list, verbatim:

Osiris by Wallis Budge
Egypt by Maspero
The Book of Job by Morris Jastrow
The Song of Songs

The Gentle Cynic
The Voyage of the Beagle by Darwin
L'Amour by Stendhal
Physiology of Marriage by Balzac
Enquiries into Plants by Theophrastes
The History of Greece
Greek Poets by John Addington Symonds
Lives of the Greek Philosophers by Diogenes Laertius
Last Essays by Eric Gill
Prolegomena to the Study of Greek Religion by Jane Harrison
Amiel's Journal
The Goncourt Journals
Imaginary Conversations by Landor

Dahlberg had no interest in mystical thinking. Myth was good, but best was the view of the naturalist, the metaphysician, and the anthropologist. I read some of the above, but concealed from him my other reading (mostly then European fiction in translation—Montale, Camus, Duras). He would have excoriated me in ways I couldn't handle. I was a sucker for bullies. I submitted, I even married them, but at least I didn't grovel or let it go on very long. Feminism was not in the minds of young women then, but it was definitely coming and overdue.

My friendship with Dahlberg ended bitterly. He chased me around his apartment on Rivington Street with his pants down, having locked the door from the inside, and I had to leap out a window to get away from him. My last letter from him was a racist diatribe against my marriage and the wasting of my "sweet, honeyed flesh."

What I received from him, before this event that ended it all, was enduring: the sense of the writer's working life as a vocation. It had requirements. You had to protect yourself from critics, and only read what he would call "ethical" writing. That is, writing that is so conscious of potential falsehoods, contradictions, and sloppiness in its grammar, it avoids becoming just one more symptom of the sick State. Dahlberg told me to take a vow of poverty if I was serious about my work. He believed in writing from the heart, not the head, and he insisted on seeking a sensuality in language that was palpable. This was his politics, he who had been a card-carrying Communist, and to this day I believe he was right. I was one more of his orphans, starved for meanings that he gave me.

"Though all day long nothing was in the ailing minds of the orphan-asylum Ishmaels but the cry for food, what these mutes ask for was never given. O Pharisee, when will you learn that we never came to your table for the gudgeons and the barley loaves?"

No matter how exaggerated, this kind of outcry of Dahlberg's was a version of my own open-mouthed horror at the world I had entered: a scabby city, crawling with homeless men, vermin, rats, garbage along the curbs, and the rich gliding past the beggars washing their car windows with gray rags. I began to realize that if I could not ascribe these difficulties to some system outside the political, I would not be able to go on.

⚘

The five years of being lost and loose were a form of nervous breakdown. I was a stranger to myself, lived as if on a mistaken planet, bathed in the orange steamy light of Titan, engaged in a prolonged and exhausting effort to understand the minds around me, doomed by a deterministic point of view. No friends or lovers could draw me into a safe space. I was not sane. I sensed I had years of drama and trauma ahead of me and never told a soul what I was going through, why I do not know. It was a mistake.

Sometimes I see on the faces of my students a look of terror that I recognize and that can be mistaken for anxiety about the story they have just handed me, or the poem. But the look has a longer history than that and can be trailed through their eyes into their memories set against their projected futures. I am not their mother. I am not their priest. I am not their counselor; I can't intrude. So I use my knowledge of tarot reading and try to read their material as if I was a medium and the work was laid out before me symbolically and we can discuss it in the workshop accordingly. Sometimes I remember my own youth in a single scene and want to weep for them. I do not expect them to tell except obliquely.

Because I don't tell. Dangerous memories are those that seem best left alone, contrary to what we are urged so often to do. If you speak of them they are deformed into words and become a potential conversation among strangers. They are not it. They are never it. They are not to be revisited. No matter how eloquent the description of the intimacy, violence, and fear, no matter how close the speaker is to what you are telling, the story is not it. Better to take up translation and turn someone else's memories into a cold poem, or better to make it fiction. True trauma has no language.

What drove "a writer of fiction" when I used to be one? It was not to pretend I was someone else in other circumstances. It was not to portray my world in mythical proportions, as Dahlberg did in his autobiography. It was the resurrection of the created but gone. The past is a fiction and the people in it; that's why they always have a story, some drama driving them around your pillow at night. So fast here and gone and chattering all along, inventing, portraying, interpreting, or threatening. The world of wakefulness itself could be read as a mass of static symbols, compared to the world of dreams, if something more didn't happen. But does it?

Most dangerous memories are shoveled into dreams, fiction, and away from heaven. They have become babble, twitches, and a plot. You can't have fiction without plot, I tell the students, but they have other teachers who say the opposite. I tell them: "It is fiction because there is cause and effect; otherwise it would be a distorted reflection of reality. It would have another name." Some of them seem to understand, to be drawn to this task of describing a circle of order in the midst of chaotic scenes. These are the ones I understand; they are closer to the problem of my generation, which dragged along with it the remnants of an idealistic, progressive social structure that would be understood through shaped literature.

※

The urge to resuscitate and order exists also in poetry, not just in fiction, which brings me back to the question of Robert Lowell, whose work and life seemed steeped in the privilege that I was born to reject. Self-loathing Bostonians are a breed unto themselves; they undermine what fascinates them. They can't get it out of their heads. We love to talk about it to each other. But why keep returning and repeating what you disdain?

Lowell's sense of history was male-made, catastrophic, heroic, European, American, a postwar narrative of disappointed overblown hopes. T. S. Eliot seems almost Marxist by comparison in his modest revulsions.

When Lowell relaxed into the sonnet form, he gave us a new kind of poetry notebook, sort of like the Arab journey poems that respond to immediate weathers, obstacles, desires, and politics. He could ride it as long as he could ride. The sonnet is like a party where you can leave when you have had enough, with a summary statement at the door of air. You are not afraid of your own absence; indeed, you enjoy providing closure. And then you can remake the whole event as you drive off alone into the night.

Lowell's sonnets, like those of George Meredith in *Modern Love,* took the personal and confessional, the ironic and late Victorian, and found enough in them to end on. Lowell is an indoor poet, unlike Hardy, whose constant experiments in the shapes and lengths of his poems reflected his engagement with weather and land.

If Lowell had written a prose memoir, it would not have been much different than his late sonnets. But by then he was being ridden by repetition. Repetition suggests an excess of confidence in the one thing you are doing. Poetry in this case.

The prose notebook is something else entirely, without repetition or revision included. It is antimemoir, a response to a day, and all the day produces by chance. It is in many ways the most radical form: a chronicle without a rhythm or a beat. Pure reflection, transparency. No audience desired or expected. It is inherently anarchist.

This might have been a liberating form for Lowell, an escape from repetition, but he didn't have time.

☀

The winters last too long where I rent a place, but the snow melts fast, the evergreens sag, the light has a short release, but the birds lead us on with their cackles and peeps recognized from the year before.

4.

When I met my second husband in Boston we circled each other while my house was being dismantled for my mother's return to Ireland and we drove around in my father's old car I had inherited from him. I sat outside many nights with the car heater on and Motown, waiting for him (twenty-four years old, a student) to come down from his mother's place, an act that he protracted as if wanting to see if I would wait or if I would be jumped and murdered. My waiting was not an act of fidelity from his point of view, but something sinister, perverse. For I was the embodiment of the untrustworthy. Just the way certain women marry and then harass a man in order to punish some other man before, I was harassed for my genetic connection to the vile actions of slave-selling merchants, their cold white women and then for the feminine in general. I could not win.

I had made yet another mistake, this time out of desperation. Unable to come to terms with the real and the social, I thought his savvy would save me. For three years I stood with my mouth open and my hands dropped to my sides: not so much a victim as a stooge: stupid, scolded, cowardly, corrected, belittled, bullied, framed, persuaded, humiliated, instructed. I was amazed that it was happening with my consent, and yet it was. In a stupor of fear, I let it happen. He did not respect a single word I said, but insisted on countering me. How I loved the story by Richard Wright, "Bright and Morning Star," where the man, the wife, and his mother are as one person, and race among them meant nothing.

For the sake of hope's survival, I became all mother to my children instead; in my servitude to them lay my liberation from him. Through them I became childish again, wandered around with disdain for the authoritarian world, left home for hours to sit in parks, sat by their beds and read to them, or pulled them into my bed to sleep in a bundle. I understood women who had many children. They accepted me, they liked to play, they were outcasts who spent their days in parks.

Roxbury was a near ruin, once respectable in the Malcolm X days of his youth, now a collection of stone projects that held families packed into two rooms, just like in Russia before Stalin came along and nationalized housing and gave people space. The city was full of talk about HUD and segregation. It was a city segregated not just by race but by ethnicity between Italians, Irish, Chinese, WASPs, Jews and then broken down into categories of money and job affiliation, so the Jewish doctors were in one place, the Jewish shopkeepers in another, et cetera. The cops were still paddies but there was a burgeoning Irish middle class and even rich elite that was beginning to take over the political reins of the city, steal them from the old WASPs, who were never very bright bulbs anyway, but canny with their own interests, like storybook foxes, self-satisfied and successful thieves.

This husband was my children's father and therefore my only husband. He was way too young for what he had taken on. An intellectual, highly nervous, he laughed a lot secretively and was eager to inflict wounds on the psyches of others. He was never boring, but he was mean. He was lecturing, but he could suddenly show kindness to strangers. Because we were bound by our shared mistake, we had a little pity for each other, a pity that approximated love. Our relationship began and ended, day after day, in a kind of fury of disappointment. Two adolescents arrested at the same point. Ideologically and emotionally stuck.

We read books with the same fervor we did when we were children. Ideas always seemed brand new. We were both equally unequipped for survival in the social and business worlds. He was a Catholic without faith but had a sentimental attachment to anything that had belonged to him in early childhood. We were often thinking of race and class, of jazz and literature, of the white audience awaiting the black writer and the co-optation of slang, song, and gesture.

Once we sat in an apartment on Columbus Avenue in New York while he was studying at Columbia's School of the Arts with Ayi Kwei Armah and Odi Okore. They discussed world politics, and things like the liberation of African nations, translation, writing for a white audience, assassination in the United States, Che Guevara, Fanon, Gutiérrez, Ivan Illich, *The Pedagogy of the Oppressed*...

We married in October 1968 and from 1968 to 1972, we had a rhythm, and a hope. But then it smashed to an end as if it had been tied to a post underwater and the strength of continual oceanic (or social) banging broke it up, and we were each tossed free to suppress the ugly memories of our days together.

Children, books, and movies would be my companions from then on.

﷼

Richard Burton, when he plays Jimmy in *Look Back in Anger*, wears his heart on his face. There is no distinguishing the scar marks, the sensitive lips, the large sorrowing eyes, the arsenal of rage that enlarges his nostrils. He can't love his wife until she is ruined, because then he can pity her. Pity is Blake's word. Who can love without pitying?

The moment he is seized by pity for her, his face is transfigured into the universal face of suffering depicted in icons of Christ. He has been a devil one minute, angelic the next. Now he is a man made of pity because his privileged wife too is finally suffering.

Nothing is as terrifying as being at the mercy of an angry man, especially when the source of the anger is oppression in the outside world. Only pity can save those who inhabit that world.

※

Charles Burnett's first movie, *Killer of Sheep,* stayed underground for far too long, like so much of the best work in film. It is a love story set against butchering sheep and their bodies in enclosures and following children hopping around the Watts section of LA; they hop from one powdery and stained building, over rusted furniture, car parts and past flying stones like children in Beirut or Palestine. Meanwhile the nearby slaughterhouse teems with blinking-eyed sheep, innocents, on their way to the knife and the camera shows them strung up and stripped of their woolen coats. They are slotted and aimed for mutilation and meat. The children are, in their way, too. This is a movie so piercing in its neonihilism (neorealism) that it is like being a killer's sleep to be watching it. Still, what is also seeping out of the wreckage? *Pity*: A child's hand stroking her father's tired face; the wife who watches her husband with a burning charity that is incomprehensible in the landscape but a proof, purely observed, of the leftover life of meaning, in this film where Dinah Washington sings "This Bitter Earth," a song that might seem like a string of clichés until you read it closely and then when you hear it sung by her. Then it is the questions of the heart that sing.

※

In the wintry light of black-and-white film one is liberated. The screen is like an artificial window speeding past a stationary train.

Through movies I entered the silver and black trees and climbed over brooks and saw cities pale and choppy on the horizon. I saw the effects of pollution in bags floating down the river and in the smog that smothers the tops of buildings. I saw human faces moving before my eyes, and they triggered expressions on the faces of all those who were in the audience watching them. I saw time loop around and backward like a flower returning to its stem, petal by petal, de-creating.

Thanks to film, we had no fear for those two hours we were alone with it. We could see the revolutionaries in the forest loading their guns, and the reactionaries in their boardrooms pointing at a map. We could see the comradeship of the partisans who were Polish, Russian, Jewish and all believed in one just world; we could see Moses climbing Mount Sinai, Malcolm X leaning forward, the crowds crossing bridges, and Cabiria drowning. We could see the loneliness of Jesus the way Pasolini saw it and the detritus of family life the way Bergman saw it. We could see Richard Burton play his voice like a fine instrument, his pockmarks and his tender eyes.

Inside your walls, film that resurrects faces and gestures long since changed or gone, that spots the shadows under the tree and the abandoned basket there, became the great art form of my time. If someone could step forth out of the screen with hand extended and offer us a sip of the cup of that silver elixir that makes the images flow, then we might drink and enter the third heaven at last. It is said that the third heaven is all light. Film is our greatest spiritual director. It shows us what it is to be a passing shadow. Inside its walls we have traveled the world and outer space.

☀

There was a time in the sixties when black artists talked with a voice that could also have belonged to all the mute animals that have been trapped, slaughtered, and eaten. They said that white artists had co-opted, stolen from them, and exploited them. Their stories and music were deformed, digested, and made into their own. They were recycled, appropriated, used up. Their hard realities were stolen for public consumption in books and bars.

Do people torment people in order to know why torment is wrong?

The artist Kara Walker has taken the dainty form of the silhouette and made it into the wildest landscape of the African American past: a rendition of slavery as pornography, the lowest common denominator, where society tends and where it finds its way again and again. Torture and oppression are forms of pornography. Sexual enslavement immediately follows an occupation by a foreign government. Cocksucking and lynching go hand in hand. This has nothing to do with sexual preference but only with power play, the play of pain's delight. Grovel, bite, enjoy, and rape. Kara Walker has devoted her time to showing us this because it is only down the street, back a little ways, near the children.

5.

In the seventies a man I knew had driven a cab around Boston in the Kennedy years. Then the Unitarian Universalists gave him a job. He was young, brilliant, persevering, sober, disabled, and black. Years later, when he hoped to write an autobiography and soon before he died in November 1998, he gave me a brief account of his childhood. We had been friends since the seventies. Our friendship began by mail and phone and had to do with piecemeal work; it was months before we even saw each other. Then we had a romance and that fell apart when he asked me to marry him. I had three children and marriage was not something I was good at. Just the possibility of such a familiar failure made me say no to him.

Years later he asked me to help him begin his story and sent me a tape that started this way: "I was born in St. Louis in 1940. Everything was segregated. My father was chief of surgery at the city's black hospital and I went to an all-black Catholic elementary school because it was better than the black public schools and because my father and mother had made a decision to become Catholics when the church became aggressive about desegregating St. Louis. . . . When I was fifteen, I had polio. My father had the vaccine in his office but it was brand new so he didn't give it to us. I had always been an athlete and one of the frustrations of being paralyzed was not having something to do. I had a lot of physical therapy and a lot of time to read. It obviously changed my life in many important ways."

When I first met this man, Henry Hampton, who was the producer of the masterpiece *Eyes on the Prize,* he was trying to raise enough money to begin work on it. He then ran a small film company called Blackside in Boston, which specialized in product training and government-sponsored films. Most of these faded off, but one, *Code Blue,* about work in an ER, circulated for many years. In 1978 he proposed a documentary on the civil rights movement, told through the eyes of the people involved at ground level, and a team of young people struck out to do research and interviews. The project was shut down a year later.

Henry shrank his company and went through a painful dry period until 1982, when he refused to let go of his original plan and attacked it from a new angle.

All told, the raising of the money and the making of the *Eyes* series (fourteen parts) took him ten years. In the process he assembled teams of advisers, fact checkers, writers, editors, archivists, and directors whom he supervised throughout each segment. Much of his time was spent fund-raising and being disappointed; but in the end he amassed enough to keep the project going.

He was a burly man with soft brown skin, a beard, and a twist to his body shape from his polio that made walking very slow and difficult. He would use canes, but never a wheelchair, unless it was to play basketball. He laughed a lot, but was more often watchful. Working with him was, for some, difficult. He was authoritarian. He oversaw every minute of production and had fixed opinions. He was loyal to friends and colleagues and his two sisters and many women tried to pin him down; one or two stayed close, but he remained fundamentally preoccupied and lived a comfortable but solitary existence. He was married to his work by the time we had reestablished our friendship.

Because he had this domestic tie to his production work, which was by nature collaborative, he was surrounded by people whom he called his family. But he could still go home and order in his dinner at night and be quiet and watch sports on TV. And that's exactly what he did.

From what I understand, the working method of people at Blackside often replicated the story of the civil rights movement that they were documenting. In this sense it was communalist.

This is what the viewer of *Eyes on the Prize* sees, a technique unlike any of the many copies that have followed. It begins with the Supreme Court's 1954 decision that outlawed school segregation, and it ends with the passage of the Voting Rights Act in 1965. A second part of the series focuses on Malcolm X, the Black Panthers, school busing, and race riots. The film footage that the production staff had decided to throw away, when the work was done, contained material from the Great Depression, the War on Poverty, Malcolm X, black arts, and religion. Luckily it was saved and is now preserved in an archive.

The final documentary has the bottom-line approach of neorealist films—the method is like a poverty that is entered into voluntarily. The photographs, interviews, and music, the raising of the funds, the turnover of directors and narrators, and different writers, all of these combined to reproduce the message of the work itself. That is, in Hampton's words, to discover how people "exist together in the same space."

He said: "The images you see are outward from the point of view of the movement in many cases towards the sheriffs, toward the riotous whites, toward the people who are precipitating violence upon the perpetrators. . . . After black power, and after those times, the cameras suddenly are now behind the police lines. They are no longer even neutral. In that sense, they have moved to a different point of view because they are frightened by the unexplained and unclear violence that they themselves in some ways have helped, not to create, but to unleash."

In the filmmaking of that period the camera descended from ladders and scaffolding and a whole new appreciation of social action emerged. The handheld camera and its black-and-white close-up footage, moving like a separate creature among crowds of people, changed the way news was experienced and reported. It was perhaps as strange as entering a continent with many countries but no borders.

There is no question that Henry's physical ordeal determined the making of this documentary as much as anything else did. He trusted people who survived despite heavy odds and people who knew how to act collectively. He saw human society from the side of those who live by quiet victories, not famous ones. He knew that local political skirmishes have the same structure as wars.

Now looking at *Eyes on the Prize,* fifteen years after it appeared and long after its events have already happened and been assimilated into our national history, I see that it is more than a documentary; it is a new art form. For one thing you get a close-up view of individuals and crowds who know nothing of what is to come, moving in one body. The streams of people crossing the Edmund Pettus Bridge are people walking blindly into what we the viewers know is going to happen. But what do they know? They seem to understand (by their actions, words, and posture) that each human person contains all that is necessary for transformation.

To film the past from ahead of it and film what you know will conclude in the present is to create and contain a prolonged now—the now of a sustained action, the now of intention, the now of resolution—like the painting *The Last Supper* or the opera *The Magic Flute.*

In another documentary that Hampton produced, *America's War on Poverty,* you can see that this so-called war during the seventies became a war on the poor, a war against the poor, a war against grassroots movements. The program raises the question: Why does the government squelch actions that are appropriate to a democracy? First it funds them, then it eliminates them—why?

We know by now that when a country bombs or occupies another country, part of the intention is to stop independent communities from developing; to split apart neighborhoods so that communication will cease and hopes for resistance will fail. This same impulse occurs at home, at local levels, with the infiltration of solidarity movements that are efforts at self-government. They are wiped out.

After the completion of *Eyes on the Prize,* Hampton spent ten years in a battle with cancer. The symptoms of polio returned. He still made more films and was preparing one on religion *(This Far by Faith)* that was fulfilled three years after he died (ironically on November 22, thirty-five years to the day after the assassination of JFK). He in all cases seemed to be committed to reproducing a revelation that he had come upon by himself and then discovered again in the faces and words of others. This relationship with the material must have been intensified by his physical affliction. He was able to manage images as if they were actions. He was able to prove, from his own invisibility in a darkroom, his conviction that all it takes to mobilize an individual is the possibility that it can happen.

Now his technique has been appropriated and watered down into sentimental pastiches on American history played over repetitive mournful saloon music. This method of making art and documentary began in the nineties and carries with it a self-important tone that is the mark of emptiness, of a producer who has not had the experience that they are appropriating from someone who has.

※

There are caterpillars that masquerade as flowers. They decorate themselves with colorful petals. They like asters and disk flowers, black-eyed Susans and goldenrod. They attach a petal to their larvae, hide, then molt and put on new flowers. Thomas Eisner tells us: "When the time comes to pupate, the larvae crawl to a site away from the flower to construct a cocoon." They make themselves a silky cover made of the same petal material and weave them into the fabric of the cocoon. "The adult that eventually emerges is a beautiful green moth, itself capable of escaping detection in a world where green is the dominant color."

6.

One day I was handed a book by a French writer from the war period. I recognized his style at once. French writers who were born in the 1920s and grew into maturity with the Second World War use sentences that are clean and sharp like a Beckett story. Each stony word makes a hard path. They remind me of the writers of my school days: Maupassant, Balzac, Zola, and Sand, who were naturalists, realists, and psychologists without the repressive instinct of the therapeutic. I can still read them in French, probably because of an impersonal note that seems prelinguistic, grave, and clear. I never stopped loving the voice of the translator as much as the original French.

Jacques Lusseyran began his life story, *And There Was Light,* translated by Elizabeth R. Cameron in 1963, this way:

"As I remember it, my story always starts out like a fairy tale, not an unusual one, but still a fairy tale. . . . I was born in 1924, on 19 September at noon, in the heart of Paris in Montmartre, between the Place Blanche and the Moulin Rouge. I was born in a modest nineteenth-century house, in a room looking out over a courtyard."

He had a loving middle-class childhood that made his days all right because of the safety his parents provided and because he knew he was happy. However, happiness and childhood were not to be his subject. It was, instead, the answer to someone's question: What are your reasons for loving life? The reasons for asking this question are one thing and his answer—his subject was light.

"I saw it everywhere I went," he writes, "and watched it by the hour. None of the rooms in our three-room apartment has remained clear in my memory. But the balcony was different, because on the balcony there was light. Impetuous as I was, I used to lean patiently on the railing and watch the light flowing over the surface of the houses in front of me and through the tunnel of the street to right and left.

"This light was not like the flow of water, but something more fleeting and numberless, for its source was everywhere. I liked seeing that the light came from nowhere in particular, but was an element just like air. . . . Radiance multiplied, reflected itself from one window to the next, from a fragment of wall to cloud above. It entered into me, became part of me. I was eating sun.

"This fascination did not stop when night fell. When I came in from outdoors in the evening, when supper was over, I found the fascination again in the dark. Darkness, for me, was still light, but in a new form and a new rhythm. It was light at a slower pace. In other words, nothing in the world, not even what I saw inside myself with closed eyelids, was outside this great miracle of light."

Then, at the age of eight, a minor accident at school rendered him totally blind. From that moment he saw no more the world he had just described to us. Instead he heard sounds he had never heard before; an avalanche of noises filled each room, and he felt people as colors that he could see interiorly. Like an alert bird, or a worm whose perceptions covered the whole of his body, he was able to hear that "sound has the same individuality as light."

He said, "My accident had thrown my head against the humming heart of things, and the heart never stopped beating."
His parents, with transcendent calm, helped him continue where he left off. It is almost as if a supernatural force suddenly gave him and his parents an assignment that they never applied for; he had to be calm, blind, and articulate so that he could witness the history that was coming their way.

He mastered Braille in six weeks and returned to school and his friends there. The family for a time lived in Toulouse, where he could freely wander in the countryside. Then they moved back to Paris, where he had a close friend named Jean with whom he did everything throughout his childhood and youth. In this friendship he developed into a social animal; there was unlimited trust exchanged in their hours spent together. The two made his blindness into an opportunity to discover the properties of the invisible. He shared all he learned with Jean and others and was followed by a parade of boys wherever he went.

The first thing he discovered, soon after his accident, was that there was a source of light that was not the sun; it hid within his body; he was flooded by it and because of it, he felt the presence of others and objects through their colors. The light in him responded to an aura of color. He could smell and taste colors and feel the shape and tone of a wall without touching it. People arrived dressed in the colors of their characters.

He never gave the light divine attributes. He did not embellish his description of it with religious language. It was not a symbol, not a myth, not magic for him. It wasn't a sign; it was as embodied as a spine. Blindness did not drive him insane, although blindness looks insane to others. People fear the blind the way they fear madness. But Lusseyran was not mad.

He lived at home in occupied Paris, passed his exams, and walked to his classes with his stick and his friends. He took philosophy, psychology, and history—the last being his favorite—while Marshal Pétain roared over loudspeakers. The French police began to imitate the Nazis. And he and his friends decided to form a resistance group made up of students.

The meetings took place in the Lusseyran family house on the boulevard Port-Royal. They called themselves the Volunteers of Liberty and he was given the task of interviewing everyone who wanted to become a Volunteer. He took his time with each interview, feeling out the timbre of the personality, the stability of the background, the nuance of the personality in the room with him. The group mimeographed a bulletin and disseminated it throughout the city. They were described as terrorists. (Nearby in her parents' apartment, Simone Weil was also writing and holding meetings.)

Though the French government denounced all such activities and paid informers to turn people in, Lusseyran kept at it. For him most importantly he planned to take the special exam to qualify for the École Normale Supérieur, but he soon learned that Nazi racial laws made students with disabilities ineligible. Deeply disappointed, Jacques became ever more involved with the Resistance and merged his group with a larger one, Défense de la France. In 1942 the Nazis ordered all French men over twenty-one to be sent to Germany as forced labor, and thousands went. The Défense de la France went deeper underground.

Then something else went terribly wrong. Lusseyran, still the one in charge of interviewing new recruits for the Défense, interviewed as a matter of course a man named Elio. During their time in the small room together, the light that usually suffused Lusseyran with the confidence to judge the quality of the person before him, failed.

He watched as something like a strip of darkness fell across his eyes, and he recoiled. Elio had a weak handshake and an unclear way of speaking. But Lusseyran let him join the Défense de la France because of his skills. Within a short time Elio had betrayed him and his friends to the Gestapo. Lusseyran was taken away and beaten but refused to name names or cooperate. And in July 1943 he was sent to Buchenwald.

Incarcerated for months and months and months, he experienced the world as he always had. There was no beginning or end to any sound, no matter how particular (a shout, a shot, a thump, a voice). They were indivisible, the way water and all its contents are. And that solid and steady light that intensified all his other senses enabled him to live an engaged life. He formed friendships, became a leader in the French Resistance inside the camps through translation and the transmission of overheard news reports in German to other prisoners. In January 1944, there were sixty thousand prisoners at Buchenwald. Six months later there were ten thousand. Lusseyran gives a full report on the months he lived there, and the people he knew and cared for, most of whom died.

"All through February," he writes, "they kept us in quarantine in crowded barracks removed from the active center of the camp. It was hard to bear because of the cold. In the dead center of Germany, near the edge of Saxony, and on the top of that high hill, fifteen hundred feet above the plain, the temperature fluctuated between five and twenty degrees below zero. . . . I must be frank. The hardest thing was not the cold, not even that. It was the men themselves, our comrades and other prisoners, all the ones sharing our miseries. Suffering had turned some into beasts. . . . Worse than the beasts were the possessed. For years the SS had so calculated the terror that either it killed or it bewitched. Hundreds of men at Buchenwald were bewitched. The harm done them was so great that it had entered into them body and soul. And now it possessed them. They were no longer victims. They were doing injury in their turn, and doing it methodically."

Near the end of his horrifying account, he tells his readers how to get through torture, through imprisonment. There are three things to remember: "The first of these is that joy does not come from outside for whatever happens to us it is within. The second truth is that light does not come to us from without. Light is in us, even if we have no eyes." The third is friendship. If you can form close human attachments to those around you, you have the possibility of surviving as a human being.

Originally typed on a Braille typewriter, Lusseyran's story unfolds as a slowly developing film, the way the light spills over a city. His blindness (the ultimate loneliness) put him in touch with the source of being. There he dwelled in a state of potentiality, in a place that precedes the blast of creation.

The blind are dependent on passing strangers in a variety of situations. A man will stop and stand on rue St. Jacques with his red-tipped stick in his hand, and he will wait until a voice comes to him, offering help. Then he will allow himself to be steered through sheets of steel and engines to get to the other side of the street. He will assent. His body will not resist or expect. He will let himself be helped by a person he will never meet again; his loneliness has made availability to friendship indispensable.

Even though the Lusseyran story insists on the existence of an interior light that affirms another source than the sun, he confesses that there were times "when the light faded, almost to the point of disappearing. It happened every time I was afraid."

※

Is life worth living when there is blindness, fear, war, torture, floods, famine, earthquakes, and prison? The answer can only be answered case by case. But one question that is also an answer might be: "Do you have your helium ready?"

A sniff of helium and you speak like a cartoon chipmunk and are gone in fifteen minutes.

Or do you prefer hemlock?
What is it anyway? It is a member of the parsley family with spotted purple stems, split leaves, and umbels of little white blossoms on it. You can turn it into a poisonous drink or use it to make paper.

Or would you be able to starve yourself? Would you have the willpower?

We have to think this way in these days of protracted old age and medical torment. The truth is, sniffing helium or sipping hemlock does not mean that there is nothing holding up the earth and the stars. It is not a sign of despair.

Everyone has the same freedom of spirit that comes with birth that she has in old age.
She will know when her time is up.

She might decide to turn the hemlock into paper and write a poem instead of dying, or write a suicide note instead of saying her prayers.

The light that is interior and at the heart of Lusseyran's story—is its point—remains inexplicable, unanalyzed, because this is the only way by which it can continue to exist.

A magician cannot be surprised by his own magic. Lusseyran can be surprised because he is not a magician. Like all people he can only be astonished by what he knows he has not accomplished.

We are buried alive in the physical world. We are the physical world. We are formed by its forms. We have light inside and all follows from that. This is, at least, what he tells us.

٭

In a castle near Loudun in France there is a gold-plated larva on a shelf. People poured the gold on top of the larva before it began work on its cocoon and so its new cocoon came out in gold leaf and the larva was shaped to that foreign substance,

shining forever as a jewel on a shelf. The larva was a living creature whose instinct for building a protective structure was
interfered with and hardened into a new material. . . . It is difficult to think about gold without thinking about light, since
both of them evade direct attention. There is no gold in the
rainbow. Light on all objects is vaguely gold; it is the equivalent
of a shadow but it is a pale shadow, its opposite. You can't look
at the same thing doing two different things in different ways.
Gold can't be found anywhere by looking around for it except in
the clouds. That's because you have to find it by seeing it in the
capaciousness of light and therefore in motion; or else see it as
something still and shining. The ring and the cloud do not ap-
pear to be the same substance at all, even if one called the tone
by the same name, gold.

7.

Snowlight on top of a crust of Buchenwald, made a plated
meadow.
Trees are like poles, leafless and unposted, but branches begin
high up, except for some blackthorn.
A mighty view through mist over a plateau to low mountains.
Entrance long and gloomy along the Road of Blood.
One enormous beige building houses a museum of artifacts and
upstairs documents.
A few rooms, where people were washed, is now a gallery of art
done in and after, on yellow parchment with pencil.
A sculpture gallery. Destroyed stuff. Photographs.

Outside the barracks have disappeared, stones mark where they
stood, and the infirmary has been reconstructed. The cremato-
rium with baths, doctors' instruments,
And ovens remains primitive, ashy, unswept.

The hill is high. A brick smokestack and then the slope goes down, down through barbed wire into the forest.

Not cold on hands but on feet. This was the men's part. The women's *hasag* was farther away. No train tracks but a little brick station beside the car park. The cells where people were tortured (iron doors, tiny windows, a wooden bench, inside some a photo of the one killed there, including one of a priest, small and real).

Time Lane is a path through the forest to the place where materials were produced by inmates.

"Despair kept him going," they said of Goethe, who sat under a tree often in the center of it all before it happened.

❦

Jedem das Seine: these are the words inscribed on the gate into Buchenwald.

I ask a foreigner there: What does that mean?
We are standing on snow and iron.

To each his own, is his reply.

To each his own?
I still don't understand. I snap a photo of part of the words to study later.

What did they have in mind when they thought of those three words? The motto sounds like a democratic ideal.

To each his own.
His own what?
Choice of a home, a partner, a nation, a perversion?

Because the motto is inscribed on the gate to a forced labor camp, I am sure its intention is cruel and cold rather than genial and philosophical.

To any prisoner—Polish, for instance—who happens to be on the outer side of the gate and doesn't speak German, it must look like a description of the arrangement inside, like "This Is Jail."

The assumption behind most prison signs is that the prisoners will only see those words once. But the guards will see them every morning and be reminded of an attitude they must sustain. It is a like a road sign that is useful to people heading in one direction only. To each his own.

No. I have nothing to say. It is beyond my understanding. Perhaps if I heard the words aloud, I would understand them.

For instance, if someone shrugged his shoulders and muttered, To each his own, referring to an unpleasant fact about human behavior, I would see that his shrug intended the tolerance that is really indifference.

In that case, the statement would be a familiar gesture rather than a threat or an economic projection.

Somehow a shrug seems like the most convincing expression of those words so far. If I think of this shrug as a bitter jerk following an observation about something unpleasant, it suddenly makes sense.

To each his own.
Maybe an ironworker was given the job at the last minute. He was told he could put whatever he wanted on that gate. So he shrugged and wrote it.

But wait. Jedem das Seine. It is a slogan with a specific cultural meaning. I have to remember that. Maybe it doesn't say at all what it seems to be saying in English, and the guy who was Russian had it wrong.
Because now I suddenly get it from the original point of view. What these words mean is, "Everyone gets what he deserves."

※

Buchenwald. Let's say three syllables or three words come out of one mouth in a sequence. They go into two ears, which receive the words as they are uttered one at a time.

Because the ear and the mind have to hear the entire sequence before they can understand it, they have to listen backward while the words enter forward.

The speaker in the meantime pushes out a sequence of syllables that plan to conclude in a complete sentence before forgetting where they began.
For instance, the nasty phrase: "Jedem das Seine."

It is strangely hard to explain this phenomenon without a diagram. Each word rushes into the air after the word Jedem. But look at them! They are in the opposite order!

If the three words were visible, the speaker would see Jedem rushing away to the right, while the others ran after.

In a poet's mind, the first word in the line is also the last. The poet's head is like everybody's, but it works as if there were no outside ears. It is as if the poet's head's ears are too near its mouth and so the sound of its own thoughts vibrates as if in a spiral shell between breath, throat, and ear. This sets the poet apart as someone lost in thought.

With a person constructing a gate, words usually thought or breathed are forged in iron, where they have no ears or mouth. They have been taken out of a context of breath and away from two speaking with one mind, away from one mind speaking to itself, and have been burned into a gate that functions like a book cover with the title *To Each His Own*. (There was such a book.)

Are written letters shadows of thoughts?
To be a ghost on the snow is to own nothing but naked intellect. Ashes, rock, solid soil, voices stopped midlife. When you visit Buchenwald in winter, you are a shadow. The snow is paper.

Abandon All Hope Ye Who Enter Here, Dante wrote on the Gate of Hell.

The Nazis could have just used that sign. But I guess someone wanted to be inventive and think up a new one: Jedem das Seine. I guess they didn't want to admit that they had created Hell by appropriating Dante's gate sign. They wanted to be ironic.

The creation of Hell is not exclusive to Nazis. Names of places over the years have come to stand, worldwide, for massacres (Bosnia, Abu Ghraib, Rwanda).

One of the identifiable factors of a massacre is that the victims can't believe what is happening to them, since they have nothing to do with the idea behind it.

They are not soldiers but civilians in the middle of their hopes. They simply can't believe it. It is like coming to understand the full meaning of the five words:

Everyone gets what he deserves.

To understand what these words mean takes as long as it lasts to get back to the day when someone said them for the first time. Listen backward long enough and you will get there. But try and stay with the present tense. It's hard!

8.

"It was only gradually that I became aware of a sense of somehow living in two dimensions of consciousness, that of the visible world of everyday life and that of another, mysterious world."

At age eight the English girl who later wrote the words above was sent (by her devout Catholic parents) to the Convent of the Sacred Heart in Roehampton to be prepared for her first sacramental communion. She didn't agree with the instruction she was given. The nuns described God in human, domesticated terms. To her mind, these sisters didn't seem to understand that God is invisible, unknowable, unnameable. Her problem with this became the subject of her life.

She followed that one issue until she died. Such a clean trajectory seems unthinkable to many of us in the modern West, so my aim in writing about her is partly driven by my own agitated questioning. Why did Sara Grant have such certainty as to live a cloistered life and devote herself to one purpose? My own youth had been a mad scramble to find a foothold in a conflicted world unravelling arbitrarily before me. For many years, as one who could not stand historical injustice, I spent my time trying to prove to myself that I was wrong to sense that this injustice was also eternal, fatal.

Sara Grant, on the other hand, spent her time trying to prove to herself that her deepest intuition, her inner compass, was right. Her strength and determination may have been largely a product of the sense of order and safety instilled in her during her childhood. Yet in either case—no matter what the upbringing—if a child feels misled by the adults in her life, this may be enough to impel her to devote herself to adjusting the error. For one child the medium for her quest might be scholarship, for another religion, for another art. Because Sara Grant was educated early on as a religious person, her commitment involved Christian theology, theory, and practice, before a twist of fate took her on a radically new path.

A few months before her nineteenth birthday, she entered the novitiate of the Sacred Heart at Kinross in Scotland. This was during the war and the school was an evacuation house that only returned to its English base in 1944. The influence of the war was kept at a safe distance, so the environment in the school was intensely closed and the house was so isolated that "the little society wholly consecrated to the glory of the Sacred Heart of Jesus and to the propagation of its worship" had unusual intellectual freedom. The convent was a teaching society, and was formed as a kind of female counterpoint to the Jesuits.

"The unifying principle and constantly recurring theme of the Constitutions," the girl wrote, "is precisely the Spirit, though in disguise, as it were; he is there like a vivifying underground stream, the living water flowing from the heart of the Lord and giving life to the Society."

The teaching instruction was of great quality, but its goal was more socially engaged than the Jesuits; it was heart-based, feeling-based, intuitive as well as practical.

Once the girl, now a young woman, asked the Mistress, Margaret Shepherd, if the incarnation of Jesus was "a means" rather than "an end" and she got an astonishing "yes." The radical idea behind this answer was one that stayed with her for her entire life: If Jesus was a means, and not an end, then he should not be an object reified and hung out like a pierced butterfly on buildings and altars, but Jesus (his life and teachings) should be a personal, mercurial guide on a path to human understanding of the mystery that is the source of being. She had finally found a teacher who agreed with her on this point; it was liberating.

She continued to attack simplistic, concrete, and physical terms for the subject she cherished. She had discovered that language could be an obstacle to reality, but it could still lead her forward. She read all of Aquinas and found in his commentaries on the Pseudo-Dionysus an apophatic theology that rang true to her. She felt that he bridged the gulf between Plato and Descartes, and she loved the sense of an eternal before and after that rolled through his writings.

At Oxford her tutor was Iris Murdoch, who took her through Greek, Latin, and philosophy. She found this intense language study to be an exercise in translation, writing that "the weekly struggle to re-think a passage from Macaulay or a Times leader in terms of the mental processes of Cicero or Demosthenes was to prove an invaluable preparation for entering into the mindset and world-view of a still more different mindset and culture."

And she quoted Augustine to show what she meant: "We think everything we say with that inner word which belongs to the language of no race of man." There is a universal language that crosses time and culture.

She began to wonder: How could a person access the language that is common to all beings, if there really is such a thing?

After Oxford, she proceeded according to plan, making her final profession of vows in Rome in 1950 and being a school-teacher and mistress of studies at home in England. During the holidays she took a five-year theology course. Her mind fulminated in a storm of conflicting thoughts, wishes, and insights. Always a person who had trouble making decisions, she was tormented by contradictions between theology and philosophy, between her own intuitions and what she was taught.

She had been sent away from home as a child. Living in a religious community was a natural way of life for her; however, she was soon restless and wanted to travel. She applied to be a volunteer sister in Brazil. Shockingly, she was ordered to India instead. It was the last place on earth she expected or wanted to go, but she decided that wherever she was on earth, she would be wrestling with the same problems and so she might as well go where she was ordered.

She arrived in Bombay in October 1956 to head the new Department of Philosophy at Sophia College. She described this period as "a rebirth" and in her memoir, made it clear, without going into it, that she first suffered some kind of breakdown on her arrival in India, even a catastrophic loss of faith in the teachings she had been given since childhood.

It was her immersion in Hinduism that she says instigated the sense of instability that was ground-shattering. Until then she had an independent intellectual life that gave her the liberty to question foundational matters. She was both safe and free in the structures of Catholic theology.

Now in India for the sake of her students, she had to enter the mind-set of a new belief system, to see it from deep inside.

She knew that there were some religions that made no distinction between the uncreated and the created worlds, a belief that totally contradicted the dualist structure that she absorbed since childhood. "All is one" was a truth she thought she had understood.

Why was it now so annihilating? Was it just because she was in India, plunged inside a new culture, or was it because nondualism made other beliefs erroneous, especially the structures of Western theology.

In any case there was no way back, once the insight had taken place in the form of a total experience, which it did. Hers was an existential, experiential epiphany.

Ironically she had sought a certain, ineffable truth since childhood (had wished for it) and now she had it.

The crisis she suffered is comparable to someone losing her eyesight. She had to feel her way forward through unfamiliar forms and behaviors.
Until she met someone else who was suffering through the same crisis with an intensity that was even more extreme, she did not talk much about it herself. Instead, she somehow turned the mental problem into an active problem and spent the next decades of her life wrestling with nondualism as a practical reality in daily life.

First she set to studying Sanskrit and Indian philosophy in order to be adequate to her students' needs. Then she became interested in founding an ashram with other religious women, most of them Anglican and Indian, not Roman Catholic. For her, the issue of translation was an extension of ecumenism.

Luckily it was the sixties everywhere. The atmosphere was wide open. Teachers like her radically changed their approach to their students and turned away from the outdated notion that they were bringing something new to them. Instead, the classroom was a site of conversation, participation, and exchange. Many dispensed with the rhetoric of the Trinity (Father, Son, and Holy Spirit) and instead spoke of creator, creation, and created.

Liberation theology with its insistence on putting theory into practice was a great help to her. She was part of that movement and its progress.

She stayed in India for the rest of her life—forty-five years.

What she set out to do was nothing less than attempt to reconcile a system that is based in language (Logos) with one that has a cosmology (Cosmos) as its source and goal.

If Copernicus, Darwin, Freud, Einstein told us what we already suspected, we still didn't need to refer to it in our daily lives. Their theories didn't change our routines. It is only the invasion of something real but unknown (unrecognizable) into our habits that alters our behavior. (Love for a stranger, illness, loss.) I think that Sara Grant may have realized that Christianity does not behave as if there is only one God since it rejects so many people of other faiths. What the Church states as the foundation of Christianity remains historically unexperienced, unexpressed.

But how ever talk about the unspeakable? The question has been asked and answers attempted forever. It lies in the realm of dangerous memories, those that are inscribed in your flesh and psyche so deeply that they have become one with your body, and can never be adequately explained.

Perhaps, since it is impossible to describe something nameless in words, an equivalent experience would have to be its opposite. One would have to describe the named without words.

She began to feel that confronting this problem had been her task from childhood. As she said in a paper she wrote, she had always been on the side of the Spirit, and the church of her time feared the Spirit. Now she was in India and so was the Spirit.

The Spirit (usually a female noun) is, in Karl Rahner's Catholic theology, "everything in the world that is constantly new and fresh, free and vital, unexpected and mighty, at once tender and strong . . . the Spirit can be perceived wherever men refuse by the grace of God to conform to legalistic mediocrity."

In liberation theology, with its Franciscan model for a fulfilled life, any person who lives "in the spirit" (that is, in giving "of oneself without seeking to find or attain to oneself, indeed to 'risk' oneself by being so generous as to freely 'belittle' oneself in regard to another person") is living a good life, whether or not that person knows anything about theology.

It was finally through her understanding of her original teacher, Aquinas, that Sara Grant was able to find a way to reconcile the two points of view—Indian and Christian. His vision was cosmological, ranging through trajectories of fate and consequence as grand and starry as the Hindu.

She was as stubborn as she had always been and persisted in her efforts to find convergent points between Catholicism and Hinduism, ultimately becoming a leading figure in the Indian-Christian dialogue and in the development of a place of shared contemplation. She became the founder and permanent presiding force in an ecumenical ashram in Pune.

Her role in the ashram was as teacher and facilitator to whom seekers would come and listen. Her ashram was ecumenical: anyone from anywhere was welcome. She had learned a great deal from one man, the French Jesuit Henri Le Saux who became known as Abishiktananda. A learned hermit, he used the term "guru" for Jesus long before she did. Both of them shared to their roots the conviction that the world and the Spirit are one in being, though the Spirit surrounds and broods over the earth. It is as if body and aura came together.

Abishiktananda grew up in Brittany and was a Catholic priest who was as fixated on the question of the relationship between Brahman and Being as she was. For years he had been in India living the life of a holy wanderer, much of the time in deepest torment. The rough honesty of his thoughts made a profound impact on her. She loved him and wrote about him after he died, which was not long after she met him.

He sat before gurus and believed that this relationship (for a Catholic) was a hermeneutical key to understanding Jesus. But again the complication was that certain other beliefs, taken for granted by Christians, become meaningless—mainly the uniqueness of Jesus—when one accepts a guru. He and she often discussed this double bind and how deep it went to the heart of the destabilization of a person seeking a truth outside the learned structures of childhood.

Meantime she, like him, wrote, attended conferences, contributed to the movement India-wide, told jokes, mimed, wrote
hymns, traveled home sometimes, and mainly ran the ashram.
A person who wants to embark on a religious life in an ashram makes almost identical vows to monks in a Benedictine
monastery—"austerity of life, abstinence, self-control, chastity
and sanctity in a life of service, housework, etc."

For her the question always remained a problem of language and
she attempted to translate the Upanishads alongside passages
from the Gospels to show where the convergences between East
and West were. But this approach became increasingly frustrat-
ing, and in the end what interested her were the different relationships between one human being and others, and between
the human being and God; this difference was a central conun-
drum. The Indian philosopher Sankara was her final object of
study and she came to agree with him, arriving at his quasi-
Buddhist position on the nature of that relationship. It was
Sankara who wrote:

> Brahman is real.
> The world is not real.
> Brahman is the world.

For Sankara there is one relationship that is nonreciprocal and
one only. It is with "the supreme transcendent Reality who created the entire universe without the help of any substance other
than Himself and entered into all beings for the sake of Self-
realization."

This Reality is more real than the world is real because the world
and the people in it are dependent on that Reality, which has
no dependence on it. Its reality is absolute; the world's reality is

contingent, one being entirely and always active in relation to something else.

(In science the term *reciprocal relationship* refers to the way that a living entity is absolutely rooted in and determined by other entities.)

Or as Simone Weil wrote, "The relative is not the opposite of the absolute; it is derived from it through a relationship which is not commutative."

As a theologian, the Sacred Heart sister wrote that "the quest for true freedom begins and ends with an experimental realization of the native contingency—illusion or non-being—of all things in themselves. . . . Without some initial touch of this experience, no human being can set out on the quest that can end only in a profound experimental realization of what in Christian terminology is traditionally described as the 'coming forth' or as Aquinas says, the 'flowing forth' of the creature from God, the universal Cause."

Over and over again she stresses the crucial factor in conversion as being experiential, or experimental. Like Simone Weil, she would recommend a life of work, out in the fields, among others, waiting. In the Western world, through the twentieth century, fewer and fewer people are interested in such attention, or labor. Even fewer are called or initiated into a traditional monastic vocation, but at the same time more and more people have chosen (or been forced) to remain outsiders, returning to rural or at least nonsuburban lands, and have become interested in questions of liberation. Human liberation requires both political and spiritual action outside of the institutional church.

The effects of uprootedness, immigration, loss of homeland and stability have created tribes of nomads, but also urban and rural solitaries who have adapted to their loneliness without being fully present anywhere. They are long-term tourists or short-term day laborers who still carry the mark of a religious tradition and desire in their bodies and a memory of childhood. They have hard lives and few priests to lean on. They have friends instead.

Working at the ashram in India, she tried to explain what it was like to be a solitary who has a cosmic sense of the Real. "Magic can serve as an apt comparison to explain what happens to us as observers of the cosmic display. We first attribute to all mundane entities, including ourselves, an independence and absoluteness which is truly illusory, but the world is not the cause of this misapprehension, only its subject-matter and occasion; indeed no magic can ever be found in its own right a cause of illusion; otherwise it would produce it even in the magician."

I first came upon her writings in a hermitage in Sonoma, California. It was lashing rain outside and a woodstove was burning. My friend the Benedictine monk was sitting on the couch and my friend the Zen Buddhist Susan was pouring us tea.
I reached up and pulled out a little thin paper book called *Towards an Alternative Theology*. On the cover was a woman in Hindu robes in a modest yoga posture.
The subtitle of the book was: *Confessions of a Non-Dualist Christian.*
Under the author's note at the front was written:

Christa Prema Seva Ashram, Pune.
September 17th, 1990.
Sara Grant, rscj

When I met her (and it was by sheer coincidence) near the millennium, she was very thin and beautiful in a sari, bare feet, with her gray hair tied back and her sun-worn face filled with curiosity. We were in Oxford in the Sacred Heart house where Iris Murdoch used to visit. She told me, with winter twigs scraping on the glass behind her head, that "the Holy Spirit is brooding, brooding" over the world.

She reminded me of a Simone Weil who might have gone to India, as her older brother André did, given the direction of Weil's thinking shortly before she died. ("Society is the cave. The way out is solitude.")

Sara Grant died a year after I met her and now I have her books and some articles she wrote. Luck defines people in the first 10 percent of their lives and again in the last. In between, they are like everyone else, struggling across the days that seem to lead to no resting place.

9.

The Abbé Dubois was born in France around 1770 and little is known about him. He was a modest priest who practiced without colleagues and lived in a foreign country, India, from 1792 to 1823. There he was well liked by the people, who considered him trustworthy enough to help him in his observations on "the character, manners and customs of the people of India, and of their institutions, religious and civil."

He learned Tamil and its literature, enough Sanskrit for his needs, wore Indian robes, visited and traveled on foot, and had his base in Madras. In the book there is a portrait of him: he has thick black eyebrows, a handsome shaven face with sensitive lips, and a long, uneven beard hanging like a bib from his chin.

He wears a turban and carries a staff. He is young, thin, and watchful. In his left hand he clutches a leather-bound book. He is what they call *Idihaya*, in India: singular, individual, unique, attentive, not divided in heart; and single in the sense of unmarried, celibate, vulnerable.

By the time he was leaving India, he was able to assert with confidence that most Hindu people would *not* be converted to Christianity. He insisted that it was a delusion to imagine that they would abandon their ancient customs and practices for Western structures that seemed to them weak and abstract.

In the process of living and learning this, and finally writing it all down, he doesn't always remain an objective critic and observer of Indian society. How can I tell? By the pleasure that his writing gives him, by the care he gives to his subject. He was a little bit in love with India. Strange is the world that reveals its feelings about itself despite its arguments.

Yet the Abbé was not won over by Hinduism (as some later missionaries would be), even while his reporting shows that he was deeply affected by aspects of it. In his book, *Hindu Manners, Customs and Ceremonies* (originally published by the Clavendon Press in 1912), he expresses in his reportage both his delight in what he saw and the need that his delight induced in him— to ridicule what he had just described. Still, he was introduced by Brahmins as a Feringhi (European) guru because of his being a respected religious, and in return he demonstrated an open-mindedness, good humor, and nearly scientific objectivity through much of his reporting.

At intervals he expresses a powerful need to defend Christianity to himself and his readers, as if he felt some threat in the culture of the people he came to know, to like, to respect, to care for in India. And he is appalled again and again by the conduct of Europeans who "have been brought up in the profession of Christianity, and who are now to be found all over India, unworthy of the faith which they are supposed to profess" and who naturally undermine any possibility of conversion.

He is scathing about various Hindu religious schools and about their practitioners who are "pretentious" and public in their displays of self-sacrifice. When he describes each school of philosophy, he does so thoroughly enough that you can see the correspondences between their schools and our own Christian sects of Lutherans, Presbyterians, Unitarians, Episcopalians, Baptists, Fundamentalists, Quakers, and Catholics both left wing and right, monastic and papist. Yet he insists that it is important to stay with the Hindu names for their ideas and not to use crossover terms, or even to imagine that it would be possible that one idea of theirs could be translated into a European language.

He didn't like any philosophy in Hinduism that suggested "there is nothing existent in the world, except the Ego." From his experience, there was a real world out there and he was in it. His favorite Hindu school was the Sankhya founded by Kapila, because it seems "less pretentious than the other schools." "It teaches," he reports, "that the soul is simply a part of God, and that the wisdom acquired by yoga or contemplation, ends in either actual or spiritual unity with God."

When Abbé Dubois told Hindu neighbors about the miracles Christ performed and about his resurrection, they were unimpressed. He quickly understood that there was nothing unusual, for them, in miracles or in people returning to life in new forms. In those days resurrections and supernatural events happened frequently among the people of India.

The Abbé admired Hindu women more than European women because of a coldness that clung to them like chastity, and he disliked Brahmin men for their entitlement, the cruelty of their assumptions of superiority. He spent a good part of the seven-hundred-page volume noticing how caste and color and religion and gender twine around each other, reproducing their attitudes at every level. Having adopted a life of voluntary poverty, he was a severe and consistent critic of the rich.

"As for myself," he writes, "for the first ten or twelve years that I was in India, I lived in such abject poverty that I had hardly sufficient means to procure the bare necessaries of life; But even then I was as happy and contented as I am now that I am better off. Besides the consolations which my religion gave me under these trying circumstances, my reason found me others in the reflection that nineteen-twentieths of the people among whom I was living were bearing far greater trials of all kinds than any that I was called on to endure."

He lists then several groups, each one in worse condition than the next, beginning with the Pariahs. There were Pallers, Puliahs, Chucklers, and Valluvas, who were called "the Brahmins of the Pariahs" because they keep to themselves as gurus and spiritual advisers.
All of these lived in desperate poverty and hunger; some of them had their homes in trees. Half of his various congregations consisted of Pariah Christians whose hovels he crawled inside, on hands and knees, and crawled out of, covered in vermin and dirt.

The Abbé retells Indian fables and folk stories in his own words and translations and describes the way notes and books are written there. A Hindu book closely resembles the work of the ancient Romans who wrote on thin boards. The Hindus wrote with an iron stylus about eight inches long. They held a palm leaf on their left hand, spread out, and pushed down the point of the stylus and dragged it from right to left until a line of writing was complete. They could walk while they wrote. Then they smeared cow dung on the leaf and washed it off until the letters were caked into legibility.

Throughout the entire volume, the Abbé Dubois excoriates the Brahmins (the equivalent of rich Republicans in America in these days). ("Shut up in their palaces, and plunged in voluptuous idleness, the Brahmins rarely give a thought to anything beyond the means of increasing their enjoyments, creating fresh amusements, and giving new zest to their passions by ever-varying means. The welfare of their people and the government of their country are very secondary considerations, if not matters of indifference.") The Abbé is an honest and self-denying priest of the type that accompanies (or used to) the church through all her most hideous histories. The tradition is loosely called Franciscan. Or it was.

In his travels he was often poorly treated by Brahmins, one of whom sent him and his servant running when the servant took a shit out in the fields not far away enough from the house. They were laughing.

I myself once knew a Brahmin.
I remember his tanned white frame. An unnaturally red lingam as short as a leech.
I remember the bulge of his chest and his two pink nipples peeping through the fur.
A self-contained belly button.
Feminine feet at the bottom of a very full frame.

White hairless ankles.
Long yellow hair, streaks of white in it, a prissy mouth.
A smell of sweet, morbidly sweet, tobacco in his bristles.
He was idle and lolled around in bed or strolled the streets with
his shoulders thrown back.
He had a heart no bigger than an Adam's apple and it seemed to
be stuck in his throat because he could not tell the truth.
He needed luxury every day and he despised "the idiots," shouted
at cab drivers and telephone operators. He required the rich to
take care of him.
He supported them with parties, cruel gossip, and time.
He believed they were more realistic than the workers who had
basically gotten what they deserved in life because they labored
for it by the hour. "What idiocy!"

Granny, you are lucky to be seated at the foot of the cliffs in a
little cottage with kettle and cups and water and bread and bed
and the sun rising through the crack in the door.

You once told me that a true Communist was the same as an
early Christian.
An early Christian lived by the Gospels, not by the laws.
Fractious caws over a mausoleum.
If you shut your eyes, your eyelids eclipse all colors and forms.
Gray matter is all you see.
It is the clay you are made of. You have to open your eyes to see
the contraptions functioning nearby. If you keep your eyes shut,
you see no eternal forms. Certainly there is no light back there.
And the memory is all in the realm of the mental, like metal
without an inscription, just a glint.

Padre, tell me more.
When you daydream, what do you see?
When you imagine, is it the same as dreaming?

When you sleep, the mental door slides back and you can see again, dancing images and colors as real as the ones outside, but untouchable, just out of reach.

But when you are awake you pray or lie in the dark with your eyes closed; it is some dark heart lodged at the back of your head that beats out a melody that seems to be visual, but is not.

Fire engine sirens are red when you hear them far away.

The siren of a police car is blue.

But if you close your eyes you only see gray.

I can only touch objects near me, but I can see the ones far away and imagine what it would be like to lean down and touch one—the gray slippery snow stack by the cement steps. I can imagine doing many things around the objects that I can see but cannot touch or smell. But how can I imagine doing things in places I cannot see, with my eyes shut even, and myself not asleep?

I think when I imagine under those conditions, I really am writing on the walls of my brain; it is only words that I am employing for imagination, not images, and these are the words that slide over the cloudy underbelly of consciousness.

I am not really visualizing what I am imagining, with my eyes closed, but am using words as substitutes for the actual perceptual things.

My eyes turn inward, so to speak, but all they find are clouds of language evoking a time and place. Invoking a time and place.

The lowest-lying form of consciousness sticks to the brain. Words, learned from babyhood, float along it. They stand in for their objects.

The troops of rain have hardened into lead.

One section thumps.

Napoleonic shouts from the redheaded grave digger: "We need more men!"

Rain, rain on a temperate silver November morning, birds' sheer white whistles.

When the Abbé Dubois returned to France to live for another twenty-five years, translating Hindu fables, he wrote: "The European Power which is now established in India is, properly speaking, supported neither by physical force nor by moral influence. It is a piece of huge, complicated machinery, moved by springs which have been arbitrarily adapted to it. Under the supremacy of the Brahmins the people of India hated their government, while they cherished and respected their rulers; under the supremacy of Europeans they hate and despise their rulers from the bottom of their hearts, while they cherish and respect their government."
His life was consistent, as far as we know.

10.

In 1987 I moved to San Diego to teach. I destroyed my home in order to save it, the way so many people do. My children were raised and now they were going away for more schooling and I had to pay for all this. With this separation, depression settled in the way a famine might; it had the force of a natural shift in potential. I locked myself up with it and my own work. A room in the building where I taught was called the Michel de Certeau Room because this great French scholar had taught here and died prematurely in Paris the year before I arrived.

I began, in the corporate atmosphere of that building, to grow interested in the new fabulous fictions called structuralism and literary theory, especially in relation to theology, and I set up my work space there. I put aside novels, except for the occasional dip back into Thomas Hardy and the Russians, and followed ideas instead of characters throughout the minds of these new French thinkers.

Outside my window were buildings being thrown together and a long view to sandy foothills and military bases. Dust and machinery banged away the days as Engineering encroached on the small space around Literature. The humanities were as imperiled on that campus as the moles and lizards and bees that inhabited the shrubs and sand. The constant threat of literature becoming extinct if classes were not filled to bursting, dominated many meetings. Even the building seemed flimsy and falling, though new, with slabs from lightweight, white popcorn ceilings dropping to the floors one by one. Yet vast steel and concrete and glass visions of modern architecture were being erected for the sciences.

Most professors worked at home, but I stayed locked in my office from 7 a.m. until 7 p.m. every day, reading, writing. The corridors were usually cryptically empty, except outside the two or three seminar rooms when students gathered. But down in one room on the ground floor was a photograph of Michel de Certeau that mysteriously impressed and comforted me three floors up. I began to read his book *The Mystic Fable*. Here the multiplicity of Jesus is scattered among many people, as if the communion wafer were a consciousness-altering drug being passed around Christian communities. His fixation on a particular kind of God madness seemed near to my own. He wrote like someone looking through the cracked window of a moving train or through a delicate web of frost.
Restless, shattered.

No matter how exciting and recognizable his passages were, I didn't dare speak of them to anyone. For one thing, no one talked about God there. For another, living imaginative writers were seen as bothersome in the Department of Literature and were not expected to have any ease with theory or cultural studies. It was a time of strange contradictions, when people who loved literature were considered reactionary and people who despised it were in the vanguard. It was so similar to what often happened in the outside world where the most revolutionary people were the quickest to judge others, I found myself stupefied by the Wonderland quality of it all. I had met many people who took drugs and criticized smokers for ruining their health. It was at this level that many department meetings proceeded. Michel de Certeau's photograph hung at a slant on the wall observing, his companion and champion beside him in the picture, and she was now a lecturer at the university. I certainly didn't dare ask her any questions about his life and his person.

Finally, years later, I found these words about him, written by her, Luce Giard, and they evoked his childhood home in a way that was sweet to me.

"Summer time would bring the whole family to their country-house near Saint-Pierre d'Albigny (Savoie), with its attached farm tended by a tenant farmer and his family. Both family's *[sic]* children would take some part in the farm's summer tasks and enjoy common outdoors activities in a combination of closeness, mutual respect, and social distance in the tradition of Ancien Régime society. . . . The house itself was a composite with some seventeenth-century buildings contiguous to a massive but harmonious fifteenth-century Charterhouse. In his late teens, he would be attracted by the Carthusian monastic life, which combines solitary life to the minimum of community links, and he would often remind friends that the order had emerged from a humble hermitage in the Alps, that the Grand Chartreuse area was close to his dear Savoy."

I learned (from her writing) that after his happy childhood, Michel de Certeau joined the Jesuits and became a scholar of Augustine, science, psychoanalysis, Lacan, Latin American history, and the devils at the Ursuline convent of Loudun. As he moved away from living the life of a religious and entered the student movements in 1968, he seems to have increased his interest in the revelations coming from mystics and mad people. Unlike Cardinal Ratzinger, he was not afraid that the ferocity of the student movement might turn into a reactionary dictatorship. He joined it. Did he remain an engaged Catholic? I don't know now and didn't know then. In his poetic essay, "White Ecstasy," you know that "the question of God" still burns in him with the intensity of a winter sun.

The Mystic Fable by de Certeau, with its erudite footnotes trailing the stories about seventeenth-century mystics in France, and his (what seemed to me) joy in the exploits of holy fools, increased my curiosity in his thoughts. I was after all a convert. I had decided to seek belief or die. That was my choice and part of my strange vocation. Others do not feel the necessity to make such a choice. I was surrounded by these who didn't, who were my "others," and to them I could not speak a syllable of what was going on in my heart.

I had been raised and continued to live among skeptics, scholars, atheists, and artists. What my conversion was meant to do was to keep me safe from irony, to keep my childhood hope intact, to allow me to live with a certain schedule that occurred outside human time. Even if my faith was on a low burn, I still went to mass. I knew that God had been proved a failure at intervening on people's behalf within my lifetime. Yet only a few

Jewish friends sat with me over this subject and entered into the wonder of disappointment, disbelief, faith, and then into texts that turned these around. Three books led me to conversion: *The Gnostic Religion* by Hans Jonas, *Major Trends in Jewish Mysticism* by Gershon Scholem, and the first half of Karl Rahner's *Foundations of Christian Faith*. And now I had found Michel de Certeau and the great thing was that I didn't have to ask anyone any questions about him or voice an opinion; it was all between me and the written page.

¥

In those years in America many poets of my generation and younger were taking lines from texts that they discovered in their scholarship and general reading. Newly awakened to the authority of the deceased, they removed these lines, like skin from a leopard, and inserted them into their own poems, or simply made whole poems out of the found words. As in the art of sampling in hip-hop and house music, the results were strangely ironic composites of the old and the new. Irony was the affect, no matter how committed the lines had been in their original context. Irony was of course the true voice of the fin de siècle as people (artists sharply attuned) felt a distance growing between their present world and the past.

In the effort to archive vocabularies, rhetorical devices, ideologies, and manners that were passing or already gone, the poets who put old texts into new forms were not unlike the scholars engaged in cultural studies and intertextual readings and cross-genre and cross-gender studies. You could say they were all of one mind, and for that time the French philosophers and critics were the gurus because they had already discovered and/or invented deconstruction and structuralism. Inevitably, in time many poets became scholars and entered the academic stream at the highest levels, seduced by the beauties of Foucault, Barthes, Derrida, and Lacan.

Why not? If I had been one of those scholar-poets, I thought I might have taken some lines from Michel de Certeau's notes on the illustrations and have turned them into a poem. The process would resemble, almost in every detail, my own usual way of writing a poem. The only difference would be where the vocabulary was found. That is, it would not have been spun from the mind that I carry around on my shoulders night and day. It would not be my own material cut from my own lineaments and hour, but from language as a general mass of available stuff.

If I were to take the words from Michel de Certeau's written notes, ones that he soberly but attentively composed (originally in French), they would of course already have a quality that was distinct from my own. He would have had no intention of seeing them become poems. So it would be a conversion of one intention into another. It would be like steering a blind man in a false direction. But there would be no denying that the material for a poem was there in de Certeau, just waiting to be run through a series of ruptures and revisions in order to compose a lyric version.

Or I could just take a line or two and insert it into a poem of mine to add authority to my private, careless epiphanies. If I did the first, turning several of his lines into a complete poem, it might exude irony; this weird, almost supernatural effect of combining your own with someone else's thoughts would be unavoidable. Whatever sweat, pulse, and blood went into the original composition of a single sentence would congeal and grow cold when that sentence was moved into a foreign system.

Let's say I take the following lines from de Certeau:

> Hair-raising visions adorn both landscape and learned
>   literature.
> The imaginary is part of history.
> Like the architecture of Callot, the writing is haunted by the
>   unstable vision
> that is mind in the spectator and object before him:
> a dangerous ambiguity between what the subject produces
> and what he perceives in the world.

And turn some of the words into a small poem:

> The mind of a spectator
> is part imaginary.
>
> Hair-raising ambiguity:
>
> Between the subject's production
> and his perception of it
> lies the haunt of an unstable history.

What would have been gained except, paradoxically, reduction? If I were to combine these lines with lines of my own invention, it would feel like adding the pelt of a fox or the limb of a hanged man to the construction of a wall.

The free-floating availability of all language (in popular culture and academic) has been drawn down into poetry by poets for good reasons and with beautiful results. Why not use it all: from technical to vernacular overheard. Take lines from the tormented dead and from mad people, drunks, captives, and foreigners whose English is ripe with useful faux pas. Sit in bus depots and barbecue pits and note down what the oblivious passersby say to each other.

Economists use the sparkly verbs of fiction to describe the economy in its daily theater of the absurd. It's like the Catholic Church with its sexual scandals and gay priests and clergy sweeping around in skirts and high hats, judging others on sexual matters. There is an unlimited store of costumes (as clothes or words) to be dragged out and reworn and flung about to distract from the nudity that is at the heart of our condition. I think it was all the talk about appropriation, exploitation, and co-optation that made me fear taking too much liberty with other texts. It is an old-fashioned and suspicious notion that I carry from the sixties. It is one of the many standards that I perhaps should discard: "Someone is being ripped off."

Michel de Certeau writes fully human, nuanced footnotes. But I have a feeling they may be hastily translated, just as the poems on the screen in Tarkovsky's film *The Mirror* are sloppily translated into English. I want to take them and remake them into even colder and more finessed notes than they are already. I don't want to put them in my poems.
I want to translate them and return them to his book.

Perhaps I am only being summoned by my nameless vocation to engender the words I use out of my own body and not to seek them elsewhere. The stunning poems that come from this other technique are already being written. I don't need to try to do them too. I am already after something else I can't explain. Should I get mad at the poets who do use material from other people's texts? No. Why should I?

Why should poets attack each other's methods and defend their own with such ferocity? The territory is small, the interest in it even smaller.

De Certeau notes: "Each one thinks he is right, without seeing that each one limps."

The night traffic veering along the highways toward the outskirts of a cold northern city, past strip malls, outlets, and gas stations must hold many imaginations, maybe an infinite potential for dreams and stories. Each is contained inside its steel machine, warm and lighted with little dials and numbers, and each contains a racing brain.

Our broken empire, America, wasn't an empire for very long. But there isn't one part of its breaking that is not also replicated in each section of the culture. In cars, traffic, movies, buses, banks, schools, war, architecture, hospitals and labs, and in poetry. If you were to mend one of these parts, it would help restore the next part over, but it would not rebuild the empire, not the same one. All you can do is stand and see where the big crack shows up in the little crack and make a note of it. Document the cracks.

❦

During his lifetime, one of de Certeau's most curious subjects was a Jesuit named Surin who wrote many books on spirituality and who exorcised one of the nuns, Jeanne des Anges, at Loudun by drawing her madness into himself. She was freed of her devils and he remained in lockup for several years. Madness is catching. Once he jumped from the window and broke his bones. But frequently he corresponded with Jeanne des Anges over the years, without anger or suspicion.

She was, I believe, what they call a borderline personality. She moved from one enthusiasm to the next without remembering; she wanted to be noticed and heard, but she didn't know the consequences of what she was saying. She was charismatic but she ruined people. She claimed to have religious insight, but she was imagining herself as an innocent at the same time.

Surin was finally saved from the madness he caught from her by a mild word from a priest and continued his life where it left off. Surin wrote a poem about being a lost child who could survive anything as long as he was surrounded by love. He and de Certeau speak for "the child of the world" who is also the child of God. I think that childhood is de Certeau's secret preserve and remember what Luce Giard wrote: "Michel de Certeau would always keep some deep feeling for the old family house, the mountainous countryside, and the happy days of childhood adventures with his siblings."

A monastery and a convent are kinds of orphanages. The church is a resting place for orphans seeking shelter and parents. I remember the end of the film *Forbidden Games* and the war orphan crying "Michel! Michel!" but Michel couldn't come and be her parent because he was just a boy.

Children are always strangers who have come from an unknown country. We soften and change our voices in an attempt to find a common sound between ourselves and infants; we gesticulate and exaggerate before them, crawl and roll around until the signals are returned. Where did the children come from, I wonder, unfurling from a seed to a sea urchin, a creature with wings or flippers, a being with smeared features and then hands. Now he is a baby, now she is a tot. Until she is seven or eight, she has her own secret. She carries it and stays at a distance with it. We have to call her out.

Then one day she discovers a baby bird has fallen from a nest; she picks it up and runs toward home to save it, but in her excitement she trips and falls and kills the bird. After that, she is one of us, fully human, not a stranger anymore. We can see it as soon as she comes in the door.

But what does fully human mean? It means that her laughter stops before it is over; she will plot her moves in advance in order to avoid feeling such shame again.

☀

In the monastery where I am now residing are about 150 sisters of Saint Benedict, almost all of them my age or older. There has been a blizzard but our rooms are warm and each electric part is functional—lights, computers, television. A very tall pale turquoise water tower stands outside with its archetypal bulb at the top of a long stalk lacking a ladder. There is a fence circling the top of it and a little red light burns there at night. But there would be no way to climb up, or to open a door without letting out a flood of water. Has it frozen inside? The fields are flat and white. They are part of the sacred ground under our feet.

I feel as if I have just arrived on a mountain plateau after a long difficult hike through changing weather conditions and have found this place full of warmth and welcome, generosity from strangers, food and light and bedding, I could be living out *Pilgrim's Progress*. The Slough of Despond lies far below, near Vanity, and I can see the Celestial joys within my vision. What is a Progress but an account of a series of pitfalls and illuminations leading to Revelation? These feelings here, where I am, are not traditional religious joys and the guide is not a guru but eternity.

☀

The third time I married is a secret and has lasted the longest. The ceremony took place in a basilica on Mission Hill on a wet Friday. It was during evening mass for the poor few gathered there, and my ceremony was a treat for everyone. People kissed and welcomed me. The rain was drenching and pounding on the stone steps outside. It was the Friday before Pentecost and the reading from Psalms was 137.

11.

One autumn, in the Chateau l'Oiron in France, near the town of Loudun, I was invited to talk about a novel of mine. The group from Poitiers around me was discussing "the secret" as an element implicit in fiction and other forms of literature. *The Deep North (Nord Profond)* was part of the discussion.

In this novel of mine I tried to use a method certain filmmakers did, having read Eisenstein's *Film Form and Film Sense* several times . . . collage, juxtaposition, interior/exterior, tracking, etc. . . . . Still I was committed to an integrated narrative, a story in this case psychological. In *The Deep North* I was writing about the formation of a political consciousness based on my own experience growing up in the United States.

In those days the daughters of radical fathers often tried to surpass them in outrage much more than their sons did. If young women suspected hypocrisy or uncertainty in their leftist fathers, they took up the radical cause with a vengeance.

By writing the story of a woman who had a history that was almost my own, I never meant to re-create my personal story and make it public. In fact, I wanted to do the opposite: to bury it with words about someone who was not me. She was prettier

and smarter than I had ever been, but she was weaker because
she lied.

Here was a female psyche in a particular historical moment (my
own) who went from privilege to voluntary poverty. I was sym-
pathetic to her, especially as she advanced toward action. The
title, *The Deep North*, came from a remark made by the Swedish
writer Gunnar Myrdal, who wondered why people talked about
the Deep South in America, when there was surely just as "deep"
a North. What was that deep place?

It was a cold society with the same prejudices as those held by
Southerners, but thoughts that manifested themselves differently, more subtly, secretively. Only by investigating this terrain
with a female character of my generation and education could I
understand it. Her environment was an ethical mess, abound-
ing in social and moral hypocrisy. Since early childhood she had
been both the victim and the witness of this hypocrisy.

As she awoke to the true extent of the problem, so did I. I could
not see a way to write her story coherently. I had in my hands a
series of discontinuous episodes, including one from her early
childhood, voice-overs, and scenes from her youth. In a gesture
of frustration I threw the pages on the floor and kicked them
around, then sat with them and moved them into a random
phalanx that went from the dining room to the front door.

Then, reverting to my interest in film techniques, I began to move
parts together according to theories of juxtaposition, montage,
close-up, and distant tracking.
Weirdly, all the material was there and more. I saw surprising
connections between one scene and another. These were un-
intended connections that created the inevitable action she takes

in the end. The pages themselves told me where they should go, the way days tell us where to go and occasionally indicate an order and a completion already innate to them.

My thoughts about her problems shifted. I saw her experience as a child as being the source of her later action. It is a scene that begins the book. One summer morning she is ordered by her master-brother to play the part of an escaping slave. She does, and in her obedience she is sexually violated by him. And seemingly she forgets what happened.

However, growing up, the child in my story becomes hyper-aware of the ways in which race, class, and sexuality are managed by the others around her. She doesn't know why, she can't remember the triggering childhood event, she cannot recognize herself as the person who knows what she knows. She is blind to the trauma of her childhood and prefers to keep it in the dark. In this sense she wants to stay like a child witness to adult behavior, to remain innocent rather than participate in learning more.

She observes poetically, in a trance. Yet even in these trances the mark of her confusion takes shape as it always does and finally forces her to see what she wants to avoid. (In some ways her trances are like subtitles in films; they are extra, outside, distractions that seem more like comments than translations.)

Despite a trained intelligence, she watches her mind breaking into parts and the vocabulary of psychotherapy driving her even farther into the pits. Psychological terminology literally makes her insane, its ugliness, its technological coldness (schizophrenia, phobia, bipolar, etc.), and does not touch on the contingencies that link her to the social realities around her.

It is during one moment, when she changes the word *depression* to the more existential word *despair,* that her confusion begins to subside. Soon after, given the opportunity, she changes her declared identity from white to black (she has a darkish complexion already) and now she is finally forced to galvanize the original source of her mania. She is able to see her white self as a sham, a costume of skin that she can just rename in order to enter the world with a different history. She is here reversing the usual story of a black woman passing for white.

Her new color lets her see the world as an invention, and people as actors and frauds. While she is now what she really feels herself to be, she is not it. An old lover returns and enters into the fantasy of her blackness as a source of sexual excitement for himself, humiliating her even further. Afterward the man exposes her lie to her friends. She heads out for the territory, as Huckleberry Finn did, with no belongings and no name.

I couldn't help remembering, when I read this paper in France, that in nearby Loudun, in the seventeenth century, those devils who were both the nuns and the people tormenting the nuns, originally went mad with desire for one priest, Grandier, a handsome womanizing priest. Their madness led to his execution.

> The body of spirituality:
> a plurality of heads and hearts in an enigmatic relation.
> Even though the tongue is the manifestation of the inner
>   movements,
> the head is deception in relation to the celestial, human
> or bestial heads that cannot be seen.
> The tongue tells the secret of multiple, hidden faces.
>
> —MICHEL DE CERTEAU, *THE POSSESSION AT LOUDUN*

The true secret of *The Deep North* is not that she tried to pass for black but that identity is deeper than any color and has its first crisis at home, in childhood. For the nuns of Loudun, it was probably the extended adolescence of community life that spread its magnificent lust around until it landed on the Father.

12.

Before the eruption of World War I, a young girl was sent to the Convent of the Sacred Heart, Roehampton, England, and had a very different experience from that of Sister Sara Grant. Her birth name was Eirene Botting, but she changed it as fast as she could. She chose a bland name that stuck.
She was a vacillator.

In her thirties, as Antonia White, she wrote her classic book *Frost in May;* it dealt with her experience at Roehampton. She wrote it in six weeks' time and knew that she would never achieve that rush of genius again.

She had remained at the convent school until she was expelled at fourteen for secretly writing a novel. This expulsion, for her equivalent to the expulsion from the paradise of childhood, haunted her for life and was based on a misunderstanding engineered by her father. After that, she was sent to a variety of schools and ended up in the mental hospital famously known as Bedlam.

"Creative joy is something I haven't felt since I was fourteen and don't expect to feel again," she remarked in later decades.

Her life was poisoned by a love-hate relationship with the Catholic Church and with her father, who was the parent who placed her, at age eight, in that place she called in her story "the Convent of the Five Wounds." He may have placed her there in order to remove her from his own temptation to sexually violate her. He certainly destabilized her emotional and mental integrity throughout her childhood, and most probably interfered with her body when she was very young.

He was a teacher of classics, an authoritarian and fussy man. She wrote of him in relation to his conversion to Catholicism: "He was conscious of something corrupt in the depths of his nature, something at once frigid, impure and violent."

And she remembered this scene with him.
"You see this ruler?" [he said].
I nodded. It was a stout yellow wooden one with spots of red on it.
"Turn around and bend over that desk. I'm going to take down your knickers and beat you with it."

Her nursery was on the ground floor of her childhood home; it adjoined her father's study with a bathroom between them. The click of his latchkey when he was coming was a subtle but recurrent sound for her.

Yet she adored him and together they ate secret sweets and went to the opera. "That was my crowning bliss," she said, "the thought that he and I were sharing something highly pleasurable from which my mother was excluded."

The problem of her father remained insoluble up to her old age when she dreamed of him doing something "obscene" to her. She had years of analysis, which did not remove the effects of his personality on hers. Her life story is a tragedy because of him and despite her great works as a writer, many lovers, husbands, two children, a deep and probing mind, and lots of devoted friends.

The father's damage was irreversible.
Why? Because it placed the source of her being in a fix, an aporia, a double bind, a bramble bush, a place where the poison and the cure were one thing. After this, how could she read any human signals without suspicion or revulsion? The truth, the whole truth was never to be her domain. The God that she feared throughout her life was a God of jealousy and love, each without limit or resolution in relation to the other. A God of judgment and an unforgiving God. She had contempt for the God of Christians who removed hell and judgment from the equation.

Perhaps as a response to her own judgments, she was for a while subsumed by the Hindu view of the cosmos and believed it was the truth, but then it folded into an episode of her madness and she had to stop thinking about the guru Meher Baba and his view of reality.

Because childhood is never repeated, there is no way to undo damage done to it. Antonia White, like so many children, was not just abused; she was confused. She believed that this fierce, judging man who hovered over her, pouring out love and attention, was the only one who really understood her. She believed he was the only one with whom she could have lived a happy life. She believed, despite her revulsion, rage, and desire to shuck him, that he was the one for her. This confusion was at her source like the smear of chaos.

It made her cruel and condescending to her mother and ruined the early childhood of her two daughters. Yet she was hardworking and committed to literature and profound self-examination and honesty, and her notebooks attest to the effort it took her to remain sane, without the availability of medication and no resort to alcohol or drugs.

She had many who loved her. But the anger that daughters feel toward their mothers can deny any possibility of her maternal charm. Sometimes the anger against the mother comes as an uncritical fixation on the father; sometimes it comes out as ridicule; sometimes disappointment; sometimes the child is like a prosecuting attorney; and sometimes the relationship involves mutual repulsion. Daughters without partners to protect them from their mothers are the most susceptible. Daughters who end up with the main burden of entertaining the mother are certain to be furious. Daughters whose careers have been stunted blame it on their mothers. Daughters who have sisters will envy them and blame the mother for one sister's superiority to the other. Was this always the case? Is it the case in other cultures, in countries oppressed and struggling? Or is it a function of middle-class anguish, instability, competition, where the mother's attempts to be fully human on her own are viewed by her daughters as outrageous public betrayals of family life?

When there is this unhappy dynamic between mother and daughter, the only one who can transform it is the child. The mother can do nothing except retreat and stay out of the daughter's way, and sometimes even end the bond by a sad distance. Only the daughter can figure out the way to redeem the relationship because the daughter is weaker.

It is strange that White's classic, *Frost in May*, written in her thirties, when she was fully aware of the significance of her traumatic childhood experience in the convent and with her father, is still often treated as a "girl's book." Interestingly she, like Weil and Grant, had a name for something that pursued each of them throughout their histories; all three called it "the beast." For Weil, it was the ruthless drive of historical forces; for Grant, it was the questing and insatiable seeker inside her; for White, it was insanity.

Yet her novels are controlled, analytical, and ecstatic; they deal in the search for eternal truths and are not reducible to an identity crisis. *Frost in May* takes place in a very specific locale and situation, but it shows all of us how during one calendar stretch in childhood our character is formed; and it is this formation (invisible to the naked eye) that describes us, along with consciousness, through every day of the rest of our life.

If Antonia White herself had been a character in one of my novels, she would have been a reincarnation of Jane Eyre, Agnes Grey, the writer Bessie Head, Anna Karenina, or Dorothea of *Middlemarch* born into the middle of the twentieth century. She would have been a social entity that cannot be absorbed into society because she is fated to observe and resist. Her story would have represented a form of human transmigration that repeats its message again and again and never has to rise, die, or circle the skies, because everything that is possible already is transcribed in her at once crossing, intersecting, blending, immersing, and being re-formed according to time and culture.

She would live again as one of my own fictional heroines because her own life was like theirs in many ways. One of them (like her in life) suffered from an untreated breakdown that followed a bad marriage to an aristocratic impotent man who inspected matter like a potential torturer.

My made-up character learned from her husband a point of view that would not go away. It was the point of view of science at its most dangerous—that is, when scientists are absolutely sure they are right about the nature of reality. (He might have touched his mother's eyeballs with a pencil to see if she had really died.)

Hope is like an amoeba: when an amoeba starts to starve, other amoebae receive the danger signal and rush to its side, climb up on it, and form a sluglike being. This slug wiggles its way to a sunny place where it grows and discards parts of itself until it can be blown away by wind and rain to green pastures to start again.

How can you describe yourself in pathological terms without going mad? Once she had been expelled from the convent school, her vocabulary had changed, and she had made the mistake of marrying a man she didn't love, Antonia White was locked up.

If she had been a character in one of my stories, there would be a long period of being chased and hounded by her beast; it would lead her through Reno, Nevada, and out again, to more men, more fear, more disappointment. She would go in and out of her mind carrying accumulated images with a depth of uncertainty that she never expressed to anyone until her loneliness was her only capital.

She wouldn't take trains, buses, elevators, stand in rooms with people, ride in cars with others, go to the bank, or eat in restaurants. She wouldn't because of the mystery of what she saw in those places and how they made her feel. Sometimes she choked, sometimes she got cramps and diarrhea, sometimes she sweated and had to go breathe fresh air. Nobody knew that she had turned into one who could not love or work.

Then she would leave (carrying *Nausea* and *Nightwood*, *The Stranger*, *Frost in May*, *Girl in Winter*, and *Giovanni's Room*) to try to see if it was possible to become a person familiar to herself. To wash away the contaminations of life in the grip of contradictions that negated all parts of her when she didn't even know it. She would have read all the long novels by then and be stuck on the short ones.

She would contemplate and even attempt suicide; many people contemplate suicide, many commit it in the ghettoes and wards and wars. They commit suicide when they cannot recognize what it is to be a human being. They cannot recognize who they are or why they look like those moving bodies around them. Children who grow up with violence do not know what kind of a world they inhabit or if they want to be there.

She was just lucky enough to believe that her visions and experience had an innate value that would finally coincide with the real and the eternal. Suicide bombers are suicides first, bombers second. Self-murder happens when the human environment is so disgraced that you can't untangle its effects except by getting rid of yourself. You forget that there is a larger body in which all of you and all of it are contained and which is the purpose of your being alive in the first place: to align yourself with what contains you.

As Eugen Rosenstock-Huessy said, "Revelation is orientation."

My reincarnating heroine would run from everywhere because she was actually looking for a recognizable truth on earth. While she would always be identified with the people who were the underdogs, the losers, the raw dealers, the young and unafraid, she was too committed to her quest to pause and fight for them.

My Antonia would go everywhere to see if her character was familiar to some invisible presence. That is: was she a creation that could survive the winds over the Atlantic and the blaring sun of the southwest?

The stranger the place, the more familiar she found herself to be.

So she would have to keep moving in order to know herself. If she didn't break apart, she was an integrated being, a pool of God, sane!

Sewn into the beautiful since childhood, alert as a fox to each innuendo of light and shade, the ideal child in a novel about school would not be twisted by rules, but by shadows and snow banks and the curling fire and the rough field grass. She would be earthly and unearthly.

The dragon of history would slap around after her wherever she went, and she could always smell his breath on the wind. But she would know how to elude him and disperse her children to elude him and they would all disappear to other places.

Now she trembled happily, finding good reasons to sit on a chunky clutter of lake with its fish spinning under the ice. Joy's footsteps were poised to fly with the lightweight tread of buntings on snow. Why else did she stare so hard at the gelatinous path of light on the ice before her? Why else would she see warnings and sighs in each crack? Every object was stuck inside space, no matter how hard it struggled to escape to another place and position.

This character knew how to identify the footprints of birds, but she knew too that they were not the cause of themselves being birds.

There was a crust of frost on the twigs and greens until afternoon.

The winter rhododendron was a brilliant pink under that icy tinge,
The holly gleamed in its prickles.
There were no temples or churches, only groves of oak and yew trees.
And a dirty hole where the seed had been.

The real Antonia White, who is not included in those writers of her generation that are taught and taken seriously, is now forever exiled to the edges of literature. Adolescence.

    ⚜

In 1932 Mary Manning, my mother, copied this paragraph into her ledger and noted that it was the theme of her play *Green Paint* (a play never to be produced). The quote was from a complex Irish writer (racist, nationalist, and imprisoned) named John Mitchel:

> To have an aim and a cause, is not this happiness? How many are there of all the human race who have faith in anything or aspirations after anything other than their daily bread and beer, their influence and social function and respectability in the eyes of the unrespectable world? Is there not a joy that colder, tamer spirits never know?

She loved a cause. These were the days when men and women still wrote love poems to each other and believed in heroic acts, leaders, and "the people." She wasn't exactly nationalist but she was cut to the culture of her country. Her novel *Mount Venus,* written when she was stuck in Buffalo in the thirties, homesick and lonely, is a story about the end of the revolutionary period in Dublin. One family, the McConnells, forms a microcosm for the opinions and actions that the Troubles called out of people.

The main character is based on Maude Gonne (and the portrait was so accurate, a lawsuit was threatened). In the novel she is an Anglo-Irish woman called the Dona, who was central to the cause of the Easter Rebellion and is now an eccentric but electrifying widow living in a broken-down house in the Dublin hills. She has three grown children still at home with her, two of them fervent rebels on the Republican side, who spent time in jail, and Liza who is beautiful, hapless, pursued by men but devoted to her family. The Dona is still a slave to the Republican cause. She can't face the weakness and slop that follow the success of the struggle in which she was immersed. Around her swarms a mix of paramours and devotees who bring varieties of havoc to the McConnell family. The novel is a study in the aftereffects of civil war.

"In the old days it had been so easy; the objective had been clear—a clean cut from the Empire and an Irish Republic based on the workers of the city and land. But now the issues extended far beyond the old creed of nationalism, far beyond mere hatred of England. This new fight had no national frontiers; it was international. . . . Marxian dialectics were incomprehensible to her fuzzy romanticism. She despised De Valera and his present government, detested England with a carefully nourished detestation, feared and mistrusted the Catholic Church. On the other hand, she was deeply contemptuous of Protestantism. She was disillusioned by the Russian experiment, but didn't know what to make of Trotsky. She had never pretended to believe in Pacifism; at the same time she loudly denounced war as stupid and unnecessary."

Mount Venus is also her only novel of longing for Ireland, and while it was published by Houghton Mifflin, it was not widely read since it carried, as did all of my mother's writing, the fatal error of foreignness. It was written, in other words, for an Irish imagination, not an American one.

In a never fully articulated way my mother stayed true to her youth and to a time (Dublin, 1916) when there were political acts that were not reduced to self-interest, graft, hypocrisy, lust, or greed. In most of her own work (both original and adaptation) there is always an innocent hero who is torn down by cynicism, and the reader and the audience are stirred by his fundamental goodness. This may be why her books and her plays are now forgotten and gone, though some day she might be included, at least, in a roster of names of her generation.

13.

One day in Ireland, during the nineties, I watched the wind roll over the shale and limestone. The walls and walls of stones were weathered and sculpted by that wind all the way to the sea. Foghorns. And around the town bright green lilting hills and huge golden trees that swabbed them.

The weather was wild: post-rain-puddle-blown-clear-winded-blue-aired. In the hotel room there were black Tudor beams, sagging white ceilings, and a pastelike wall. Again, red beech leaves were swaying against the window. It was a blackish red that reminded me of something lost in my childhood.

If I looked at it hard, my eyes started to cry. Trucks rumbled past and shook the panes.

On that day an early darkness wrapped itself in voluminous clouds. The forecast was for sun, showers, heavy rain at times, clear, clouds, and drizzle. Someone on the radio referred to "the common people of Derry" as the ones who marry after being in trouble for acts they didn't commit.

Someone else said the Downing Street Declaration should be treated as a literary document, so that scholars could come and interpret it. She said no one trusts the rhetoric of politicians, but they do trust the language of poetry and literature. "Politicians are viewed as despised agents."

In Belfast the people murmured about how the children were becoming monsters.

I parked near the border and listened to a political analyst list the qualities of a true enemy:

—knows you personally and doesn't care if you live or die
—talks harshly about you behind your back
—sees you as a symbol rather than a whole
—wants more from you than wants a fair exchange be-
    tween you
—exaggerates your flaws in order to get others to hate you
—wishes you ill in work and home life
—has the desire for something you have
—has contempt for your intelligence and too much belief
    in his own

If someone is in fact your enemy you can decide to be ene-mies of each other, hate each other without guilt, and then kill what you hate: hate itself. The lovers on the sidelines will have to avenge each one of you and turn their grief to hate. . . . Children are very susceptible to hate yet in them it burns away quickly. It is only later that it organizes itself into a system, a way of life.

I wondered: Maybe that hedge is not a fence but a wicker chair turned on its side?

For what does it mean to "believe in" something?

I realized that it simply means that you are conscious of the potential for something to become new.

※

Hills where sheep are lolling in the mud, hedges like twine, on the way to somewhere by air and spirit. Topiaries are mysterious creations—wire and twine with vines for skin. Hunters must have invented them for games. Another stone city, then home and on with the treks across the heath. And the surrounding transparency, including myself, increases as my escape from this pattern approaches.

Yorkshire's land seems like a rolled-out textile, flat and thick. Charlotte Brontë's unborn baby's lace cap sat on the father's bed for a little too long a time in my imagination.

Can a person visualize geological structures in three dimensions from on top of the earth. Some authorities say that Emily Brontë in her "lost year" gave birth to her father's child.

Incest was not an unknown subject to her, but how can we know if she had experienced it?

History seems to grind out the same grid and hole in the textbooks. In one lifetime, there are endings and beginnings to relationships that are astonishingly repetitive. Female history is like a father who makes his daughter pregnant.

Northern Ireland, for instance, is contradictory like that: February, when the sky is staying light until nearly 6 p.m. already. There are large fat sheep grazing on the slopes. Then stern stone houses facing west and an English feel to the landscape that is very kempt and green with oaks bursting out of the soil like houses without architects.

Patrick Brontë came from this soil and moved to England to put his religious practice to work. That was almost two centuries ago. He was born in County Down, educated himself, did very well, and attended Cambridge University in England. He was an Irish Anglican and a poet. At Cambridge he changed his name from Brunty to Brontë, which means "thunder" in Greek. He had red hair and was a Tory. His novel, *The Maid of Killarny*, was published the year Emily was born, 1818.

Into the 1960s Belfast was seen as far superior to Dublin in terms of industry and good sense about money. There was interesting theater and a literary life. Belfast was seen as superior to the Republic in terms of Western civilization and its highest goals; then the violence began and the verdict changed.

When you cross back down into southern Ireland, the atmosphere and even the sky itself seem to change into a different substance. A less territorial feel to the hills and valleys, more rambling and toss. More fun, as when you pass from the gates leaving the UK at Heathrow and enter the Irish section of the departure. The walls and floors are identical. But the swelling in the air is less predictable and more elastic. People move differently; there are unruly children and baby-faced men.

People who are destabilized by historical forces are more intelligent than the secure ones who have got the formulas in place. The safety of received tastes and opinions, confirmed in furniture and inherited artworks, stops the true brain, the brain of the seeking blind. When people are uprooted and insecure, their tables are alive with the conversation of prophets—philosophy, music, literature, God. But when the people are safe, the repetition of a formula goes around and around.

☀

Emily Brontë was thirty when she wrote her last poem, and soon after she died from a cold contracted at the funeral of her brother, who was also thirty. Her cold turned into consumption, and she refused medicine, food, or comfort, continued her daily tasks, and cooperated with her illness fully until it took her away. Like Simone Weil, she had tuberculosis and died of self-starvation.

A few of her siblings had already had tuberculosis. She was the fifth of six children in the family, three of them passed away early; her mother had died when Emily was a child. Her father was highly sexed but lonely, tender and involved with his children, an inspiring preacher and a writer. He made sure his children were highly educated, could play the piano and paint. So they spent the time they had free as children doing these activities and writing tiny books together. He would go out and shoot his gun at night at the parsonage walls, and in between he proposed to several women who rejected him. His agitation was ceaseless.

Since stone was part of the outdoor world, Emily was at ease with the cemetery eating away at the walls of the parsonage in which she lived. But it was the moors where she walked a good part of each day that gave her both a heathen and a transcendent spirit, the split consciousness that tore at her novel and poems. As splits will do, this one split into more splits and fragments and frail portions of selfhood. She had her characters in her stories that she wrote as a child represent parts of the world she knew, and above all Heathcliff and Cathy in *Wuthering Heights,* who were one person broken apart, never able to return to the union they enjoyed as children, not through sex or fantasy, thanks to timing and other people. When they died the locals saw them walking the moors together again now as specters in the night.

Brontë was in her work and her life committed to one vision. It was pantheism inspired by metaphysics, metaphysics inspired by pantheism. This was many decades before mass war and nihilism. Living in the wilds as she did, it was possible to know that there was no difference for her between this and the other world.

Only someone who insists on saving her childhood from developers and clerics can experience the phenomenon of fusion. The saved childhood is the key.

She continued to write her little Gondal books until she died, whereas her sisters and brother stopped. Out of these books she drew some of her greatest poems. But the last poem she would ever write exists with the clarity of its solitude (outside fiction) like an Upanishad. That is, it reads like something that was always written. Why? Because it seems generated rather than produced by thought, it moves as fast as its thought and declares, from its first line on, its freedom from fear.

> No coward soul is mine,
> No trembler in the world's storm-troubled sphere:
> I see Heaven's glories shine,
> And faith shines equal, arming me from fear.

If the world and heaven are the same phenomenon, then there is no way to escape them, not even by dying.

There is not room for Death,
Nor atom that his might could render void:
Thou—Thou are Being and Breath,
And what Thou art may never be destroyed.

☩

Often a poet will use repetition by *not* repeating the same word in one poem. Instead the poet will *almost* repeat or rhyme a sound but not quite. *Almost* suggests there is a margin of uncertainty around your thinking. It reminds you that there are echoes that bounce up and away and all is wildness.

Repetition on the other hand (whether by chorus or by word) comforts the memory, and makes the objective world seem systematic and safe. The hope is that something good in this life will be repeated perfectly some day.

Religious ceremony repeats, word for word, the same sentences and gestures and in this way it seals off the margin of uncertainty. In church, repeating again and again the liturgy of the Word and then of the Eucharist, you become soothed by their familiarity. Saying the same things again and again deepens your assurance that some things last.

Revision is the opposite of repetition and religion. In the process of stripping the language back to an unnaturally naked state, you want to see what is hidden behind each word, what intention, what fact, then cover it up with something else. Revision is suspicious of first words and assumes they exist only to signal something else, something deeper. I revise what I have written in order to strip away fraud and get to the uncontaminated first intention. By slashing the curtains of words, I might finally glimpse the words behind the words and the silence behind those.

In Emily Brontë's poem, she streams out syllables of varying sounds and beats, sounds that continuously suggest a possible resting place but don't find it: that is, not until at last she repeats one word: Thou! It is the resting place.

※

It was thankfully a windy fall gold day when I was at last going to visit the Brontë house. Smell of manure dense and goats among the fallen leaves. At the parsonage, there were the graves lined up eating the ground outside with the smell of a crypt or the streets of the East Village after 9/11, and inside the tiny clean rooms a sense of intense intimacy, holing up.

They were a close family, though one after the other died, beginning with their mother, early. Beds and graves had barely inches between them. "The Visionary":

> Silent is the House: all are laid asleep;
> One, alone, looks out o'er the snow wreaths deep;
> Watching every cloud, dreading every breeze
> That whirls the 'wildering drifts and bends the groaning trees.

> Cheerful is the hearth, soft the matted floor;
> Not one shivering gust creeps through pane or door;
> The little lamp burns straight, its rays shoot strong and far;
> I trim it well to be the Wanderer's guiding-star.

The visionary lights a lamp for others; the visionary is fortunate to be safe at home, taken care of, not thrown into alien spaces: classroom or train depot. The visionary is lucky not to live among worldly people who eat books greedily and spit them out when they are not interesting to them. But the visionary is able to be the Wanderer, too, cold in the snow, looking at herself staring out of the window with the candle lit. What you seek is what you find because it is already in you as an image.

⚹

Who would dare be a visionary while staring out an icy train window on the way to the 125th Street station, with work to do, people to face, converse with, speak honestly to? Well, there are such visionaries. Poets and singers who have scrambled up the wrought-iron steps and down again along the edges of buildings and elevated trains. Drunks shouting up in that false female chord they do. And the snow coming down, floating over Fifth Avenue, solid white, impenetrable by car, all of us on foot, leaving Harlem midwinter, without boots or mittens or hats, so clutching each other by hand and in pocket, this was years ago, when we shared our vision in the snow and piled down the center of the avenue, while the streetlights sparkled and squinted at the fairylike drifts. Snow-sprays instead of May-sprays on the branches in Central Park . . .

We move forward into a past that will be censored.
This is the way we follow our friends through the night, no one leading, no one speaking because of the ice forming on our lips and our eyes burning from our freezing lashes. We intuit our best path and sustain our belief in finding warmth by physical touch. All that we know of each other is in this sudden storm useless, limiting us to memories that were born in comfort. The trail of our footsteps is eliminated by the deepening snow. It would make no sense to look back. What would we see but the same as we see ahead? What can we take for granted?

That we will lean together for warmth until we find a way inside a building. That we will form one creature out of our many limbs and torsos, coats and shoes, by sticking to each other, and never speaking. We are all atheists, truly modern people, literate and skeptical. We all like to dance and to laugh, to drink too much and to neck rather than fornicate. We are young in a snowstorm leaving Harlem for downtown.

☘

Once Brontë has written "No Coward Soul Is Mine," she is naked. The stripping bare unfolds with each stanza's completion and the final glance back at the end that is animal and vulnerable; after all, now the confession is irreversible.

What triggered the opening line?
Her older sister Charlotte might have called her a coward, or suggested it, when Emily insisted she would die standing up rather than have medical treatment. Maybe her brother had died as a coward and she wanted to outdo him.
More likely, she wrote this poem quietly in private, on her feet, while she was dying, and it is addressed to God so God will recognize her when she falls.

Emily, shy and stubborn and unable to leave her childhood behind, was in a worldly sense a failure. She couldn't leave home. She slept alone at night. She had a dog. She read a lot and played music on the piano. And then there were the moors outside where she had her daily walks.

> With wide-embracing love
> Thy Spirit animates eternal years,
> Pervades and broods above,
> Changes, sustains, dissolves, creates, and rears.

Though earth and man were gone,
And suns and universes ceased to be,
And Thou were left alone,
Every existence would exist in Thee.

To feel like a failure is to feel the pain of leaving potential behind and then give it another name, failure, which still involves you although you are of no importance. To feel the way Emily Brontë did when she wrote these lines is to fail to resist dying; she had the spirit of the Hindu poet Tagore when he wrote:

You are the ultimate Rest unbounded:
You have spread your form of love throughout the world.
From that ray which is Truth, streams of new forms are
    perpetually springing
And you preface those forms.
There the Eternal Fountain is playing its endless life-streams
    of birth and death.
They call him emptiness who is the Truth of truths . . .

Waters Wide

The Teacher

Memory will tell me if I remember
The trauma of that day. The driveway
To the house that ended at the garage
Instead of the door and the boy

Who froze on a field of snow.
The deer in the garden up to seventeen
At a time, picked at the ice-cold boughs.
I couldn't lift a shovel or the knob

Underneath the cement steps with the bag
Of salt where the children came in.
I'd haul wood up from the basement
To light a fire every Wednesday night.

There were twelve brown and rosy children
Their faces in the lamplight were anxious
For me to read aloud to them. Poems.
I had an electric pad in my bed and my dog

And I walked a lot along along
The river bank. She ran fast and once
We saw a deer hanging on a branch.
The deer stayed there frozen and brown

All the winter even into May.

I realized many things I remember
Having thought before and have now forgotten.
But I do remember the day the hound and I
Walked along the river and the still

Drab branches pierced the hillside like thorns
And the certainty of my revelation
About time caused vertigo. I never would be the same.
But still I went home to watch a film

Dreading the end of it and loneliness.
The red cardinals in the morning and evening
Had a piercing whistle like a beak in a berry.
Then the light changed and buds began

And I drove east, the trauma fixed in place.
That place, that walk, that season.

⚐

Not long ago I realized I was wrong about the relationship between the world and time. This revelation came to me walking on a path alone on an ordinary winter day, and it needs no description except to say I stepped into eternity beside a river in Ohio.

Later I went to visit my friend, a Benedictine monk from Sonoma, California. I tried to act out my experience on a small rug before his feet, to show him the way it felt to step into eternity, because I couldn't shake the experience. He only said: "Maybe you should read Bhartrhari." And he spelled the name for me.

Who was Bhartrhari?
An Indian grammarian who wrote in Sanskrit in the fifth century. One who believed that "grammar leads to God."
He was, people think, also a poet by the same name, but this can't be proved.
He and his fellow scholars were seekers of a truth in an elsewhere beyond language. They used words only as a trail to the enlightenment they sought.

If they could understand the origin of language, they could understand the origin of the universe.
Bhartrhari wrote what was called the Sphota theory. In a nutshell this theory maintains that the uttered word has one purpose: to

reveal the inner, unspoken word's meaning. This inner word, which precedes any articulation, is the object of speaking.
It has a unity that precedes sound. However, to discover the word's unity, one must speak it, release it into the air.
When you are about to speak, you formulate your sentence near the back of your mouth. That chasm is the color of clay but cloudlike, active. The words take shape there on the cusp of sound and silence.

Bhartrhari described four levels of language, beginning with the least significant:

The articulated one (external and audible)
The middle one (mental and potential)
The witnessing one (latent and formless)
The supreme attendant (fundamental to being and transcendental)

He said that these levels correspond to levels of self-realization.

The written word is inferior to the spoken word because it is unable to produce the kind of nuanced music that the breath gives to speech; and likewise the spoken word is less significant than the potential but unspoken word because it is farther away from its origin.

Between the potential word and the origin, there is a watcher: consciousness that broods over every utterance, thought, and dream.
It is similar to a sky that fulminates with gray and pale-colored clouds, a lighter form of water that broods and vanishes into the blue.

Like Virginia Woolf's description at the beginning of *The Waves*: "The surface of the sea slowly became transparent and lay rippling and sparkling until the dark stripes were almost rubbed out. Slowly the arm that held the lamp raised it higher and then higher until a broad flame became visible; an arc of fire burnt on the rim of the horizon, and all round it the sea blazed gold."

Bhartrhari was determined to show in his study of linguistics that the meaning of each word in a speaker's mind already exists in the mind of the person hearing that word.

How else could it be? If the mind is not differentiated into sounded and formed words before they are uttered, how could they form coherent units only when they are spoken?

If a thought only breaks into intelligible language when it is uttered aloud, how does another person, listening, recognize that language? Mustn't the listener already have the same word formed in her mind?

Bhartrhari believes that the listener waits in full knowledge of each word coming. He is like someone watching a distant figure who draws closer and closer until he is someone recognizable.
The listener has the potential to understand the words that his neighbor is about to speak to him. These words are not fully formed as he waits to hear them, but when he hears them, they take on a structure that is recognizable to something already in his mind.

Each person is born with a store of potential words, which are affected by the culture she grows in; the words exist as universal types. Consciousness is silent, but thoughts that are potential words acquire personality through articulation and their cultural habitat.

(A yogi who meditated without cease for a hundred years asks the Lord one question when he finally appears to him. "Why did you take so long coming?" "I was always here," is the answer.)

The whole word is of greater value than all of these modulations and all the letters put together. The word is proof that the mind exists, the latent and formless one is ready and waiting. It is ununconscious.

There is an underlying language born in and with the minds of all people, expressing and shaping itself according to culture. There is a prototype for every word; otherwise there could not be communication, and everyone would be insane.

Even the young Wittgenstein wrote:

"There is not—as I used to believe—a primary language as opposed to our ordinary language, the 'secondary' one. But one could speak of a primary language as opposed to ours in so far as the former would not permit any way of expressing a preference for certain phenomena over others; it would have to be, so to speak, absolutely impartial."

Bhartrhari believed that the single letters that compose the prototypical word do not have a typical meaning but only the complete word does. This is why letters differ in so many cultures.
The latent and potential word is hidden until the letters have been configured to produce it.
The formed word, articulated, then has to be sounded to exist at all.
Pitch, modulation, object, intention, culture—these alter the way a word is heard when uttered.

A listener assesses spoken words before making the final judgment, in the spirit of one seeking a truth. The listener hears the words coming in the opposite direction from the speaker: the first becomes last. The speaker's words echo or operate like a mirror on the listener.

Bhartrhari would say that the words only acquire their meaning in a relationship of exchange. The listener is the one who makes sense of the utterance, who catches it and finds it recognizable or not.
Without two people, there could not be one word. The future is like a listener who can put the sounds together and respond. The future is only the past recognizing itself at another location.

The world as the site of salvation is all that interests Bhartrhari, because it is where you put your feet down and strike what is real.

He had a practical and cyclical view of creation, rather than a linear one: there is no beginning or end but a series of continual regenerations. His was an agricultural reading of creation.

(The horses ford the brook at six, the midges emerge at eight, the rooster returns to his coop, the fish sink in the pond, and the flower petals fold in. The proboscis is used as a straw for drinking nectar, and some insects lean over and salt their eggs.)

He studied language as a way to liberate people from feeling alien. In his time all disciplines were yogic disciplines. Yoga was not limited to physical stretch and breath; every kind of work performed for self-realization was yoga. This would include the arts, the sciences, and forms of manual labor.

He believed in the immortal soul and he was a pragmatist.

His study of language taught him that a person is born with linguistic intuition, inherited from earlier generations. All the properties of a thing are reducible to its relations within a system.

Jacques Lusseyran said about living in Buchenwald: "[This] is what you had to do to live in the camp: be engaged, not live for yourself alone. The self-centered life has no place in the world of the deported. You must go beyond it, lay hold on something outside yourself. Never mind how: by prayer if you know how to pray; through another man's warmth which communicates with yours, or through yours which you pass on to him; or simply by no longer being greedy."

Walt Whitman shows that in poetic thinking, the ideas that triggered the poem are never stated, exist only in the past, and are never introduced into the poem as its subject. Instead the poem arrives as an effect of these ideas and as a result of discarding many possibilities.

Bhartrhari puts it this way: "By treading the path of untruth, one attains truth."

What is heard is what is past. What is seen is what is past. The listener and the witness are the future in the present.
And the past you just had is erased forever. None of the words for time (past, present, future) have a reality beyond their usefulness for performing tasks on earth or in sentences.

I walk down a busy street and every face has completed its task, and is walking from that completion toward the future I represent, my present. I look at you coming and I see you rising out of your ended tasks and I must touch you in passing, must kiss your cheek as we both disappear into each other's trail.

What I realized on that day in Ohio is that the created world is here and finished. Now we are walking around on creation. And since it is finished, it is the site of eternity. This is why we can still make it glorious and productive while we wait and watch.

A prayer to an angel reveals the force of two-way time: "O Raphael, lead us toward those we are waiting for, those who are waiting for us; Raphael, Angel of happy meeting, lead us by the hand toward those we are looking for."

⚡

It is only in the act of working on something, be it manual or mental labor, that you are aware of being at least half at the mercy of a will that is not personal, is not your own. You even appeal to this will, under many different names, for help and concentration, for justice and a beneficial outcome. You are both seized and suffused by this will that is an impersonal version of your own existence. It is like a translator who holds a position both behind and in front of you, both in your past and in your future, who strips away the attributes of history and culture to find some primordial language that belongs to you and everyone else.

When you call on this presence for help, it is then as if you are an underwater diver whose rope attached to the boat has broken. You call for help to have the rope tighten again. It is a realignment and a tug from the source upon which you are absolutely dependent. Some people call it a plumbline. I know what they mean when I am on dry land, lost, and feel something loosen, a line that runs from way behind to way before and to way above. It might be a light beam, the kind that bends to gravity. But it runs through me and on it I am utterly dependent. Why name it? Why praise it? Why sing to it? Why tame it and bring it into the common tongue for discussion? You know why most ardently when you are at a certain level of suffering, especially from self-loathing, and you see the face of the Theotokos painted on the rounded dome in Byzantine cubes, available to everyone. It is what it is.

God is unevolved and therefore cannot be apprehended by the senses, and so God exists as the witness of what is and also as light and energy, neither of which can be touched except by touching itself.
You put your hand to your cheek and touch your own light and your own energy.

You can call light and energy by the name of God if you want.

If you don't want to say God, you must expect this choice to help make you lose your bearings until you understand how it moves around, shifting its position from being in you and of you, to being far from you.
Divinity—Trinity—What's the difference?

No difference? No difference, no words. No word for difference, no identity. The genealogical and psychological search for an identity hitherto unnoticed, unknown, leads nowhere. The world is the unconscious but nature is not symbolic.

There is nothing inside or outside us to be identified as being our real self.
We have no identity in the sense that we are looking for one. Emerson noted, we and the world are all surface, surface, surface, but is this so?

The quest for a condition that exists in two separate states is what confuses people. The person looking for "me" (a fixed iden-

166 The Winter Sun

tity) is also the same person looking for (a vapory word) "God."
This split search can only be folded into one in the process of
working on something—whether it is writing, digging, planting, painting, teaching—with a wholeheartedness that qualifies
as complete attention. In such a state, you find yourself depending on chance or grace to supply you with the focus to complete
what you are doing. Your work is practical, but your relationship
to it is illogical in the range of its possible errors and failures.
You align yourself with something behind and ahead and above
you that is geometric in nature; you lean on its assistance.

≱

Simone Weil said in "Human Personality":

> At the very best, a mind enclosed in language is in prison. It is
> limited to the number of relations which words can make si-
> multaneously present to it; and remains in ignorance of thoughts
> which involve the combination of a greater number. . . . The intel-
> ligent man who is proud of his intelligence is like a condemned
> man who is proud of his large cell.

Yes, the problem of vocabulary in these matters is obvious, because a solution to the problem is made of the words. Who
doesn't know that? If a bird has a problem with its whistle, it has
to whistle to fix it.

All voices tend toward song, and the vibrations of music in the
vocal cords deeply influence the way spoken words are heard.

Franz Rosenzweig noted: "In actual conversation something
happens. I do not know in advance what the other will say to me
because I myself do not even know what I am going to say, perhaps not even whether I am going to say anything at all. . . . To

need time means being able to anticipate nothing, having to wait for everything, being dependent on the other for one's own."

I understand that what is heard is what is already in the past and the proof for that is measurable. Sound has to travel a little way; it has to overcome space in order to reach a pair of ears. In this space of time, a few distortions can occur. Anxiety, misunderstanding can intervene, even heartbreak. Indeed, words themselves can, if allowed, seem to lose their original intention on their way out of the mouth.

Socrates believed that the soul is eternal and contains knowledge of all things. In the trauma of birth, the soul loses its memory and has to start all over again. But in the experience of living and learning, it finds its way back to the truths that it lost.

⚇

Revision is the path taken by an autodidact like me. In revising you teach yourself. You find your own information buried in your body. It is still alive until you are not.
Right until he committed suicide in the end, Socrates had the high spirits of someone who knew (as in recognized) himself (his own condition).

One way to understand your own condition is to write something and spend a long time revising it. The errors, the hits and misses, the excess—erase them all.
Now read what you have rewritten out loud in front of some other people. They will hear something that you didn't say aloud.
They will hear what was there before you began revising and even before the words were written down. You won't hear anything but the humming of your own vocal cords.

It's the same as what Remy de Gourmont in his "Dust for Sparrows" wrote from the point of view of the listener: "Never have literary works seemed so beautiful to me as when at a theatre or in reading, because of lack of habit or lacking a complete knowledge of the language, I lost the meaning of many phrases. This threw about them a light veil of somewhat silvery shadow, making the poetry more purely musical, more ethereal."

Even while I have gone back over the words, I have never been sure of the need for it, the use of writing at all, the value of any completed poem, or the idea that writing might lead somewhere. I haven't really known what I was doing, only that I would keep on doing it. It is a form of promiscuity and wanderlust. I could just as well have been a barmaid or a mailman. I could just as well throw all these papers in a river before sniffing some helium and letting go, because it was in the end only a part of the natural world.

⚜

A Benedictine friend said there are three levels to transreligious experience: "My religion is best." The second level: "All religions are the same." And the third level that changes the first two: "Through a deep reading of my own tradition, I find that all religious traditions converge."
Likewise, through a deeper reading of my own language, I should be able to uncover a few words that correspond to certain transcendent words in other cultures.

I shouldn't need to co-opt words like *Brahman* and *atman,* no matter how much I am drawn to them and the novelty of their sound.
I must find in English the words that bear the same force as those two do and share their meaning. This is my job.

⚜

The worst sinners are the clerics who give God human attributes. Humans after all evolved from being slime into being
beasts, and like all creatures, it was fear that drove us to change
our form over time. Fear of being devoured, swallowed, and
turned back into slime. Watch the scaled animal turn into a
bird out of sheer terror, and you will see what humans went
through, too. Humans are still formed from those evolutionary
stages and revert to bestial behavior when threatened.

Even if all of evolution happened, from the eye of eternity, in
one wink, as a swift unveiling to the present day, this movement
would be nothing like the stillness of God. This stillness is not
something you come to, after years of struggle, or learn about,
then encounter, or find refuge in, after a fight. It doesn't await
you in a specific location.
God is always in the same everyplace, without an adjective, an
adverb, or a verb tense. A baboon has knowledge of God just as
a bee does, and a human child or a leaf.

Fear is what holds humans back from evolving to full solidarity.
Providing safety for people—it has to be an action for all people,
this is the difficulty.
Everyone has to be safe for everyone to be safe. This is the mes-
sianic message.

There are people like me who read a love letter over and over
again. Every time they see a different message and a different
level of love, until they have read it backward and forward several times, and deemphasize certain words. In fact, they cannot rest.

For these people sound is eternal, it has no beginning or end.
For others, the search for the right word produces a conclusion
to a beginning.
In both cases, happiness is the goal.

Will I be happier if I call God Brahman?
Will I be happier if I call God Divine?
Will I be happier if I study the Trinity?
Will I be happier if I discard the concept of both One and Three
and head toward the Zero that is emptiness for Buddhists and
fullness for Hindus?
I will only be happier if I write a poem.

> The trees billow under a vague gray sky.
> Nearby and not far away, suffering.
>   And the end of me.
> But if I know I have everything
>   Then I can begin.
> Lucky to enter completion conscious.
> Lucky to be well. To have my cell.
> Wine, words, wafer, in all their forms.

⸎

The winter has returned. The warmth that signaled spring
has been replaced by an angry frost. The arms of the pines lift
and drop in concession to a low wind. This is tornado country. People have basements to hide in. If a water tower gets hit,
surely it tips over and out comes a geyser. Someone only yes-
terday told me that the harm we have done to the world is now
irreversible. At the same time we can finally look through a tele-
scope strong enough to see the beginning of the universe. It is
not a beginning if it can be seen still happening from where we
stand on earth. The cardinal whistles at the top of a spectral
elm, or is someone writing on a slate of air?

⸎

Without the children, there is only one reason to live and it is
the same reason that justifies having children in the first place.

Perhaps it is the only justifiable reason to have life: to see and to be.

There we will create a little home school and theater and call it the world.

One child is my right eye, the boy, when I am looking at my face onstage.

The other child is my left eye, this is the first girl.

The third child is my mouth, this is the second boy.

The fourth child is my right ear and the fifth is my left.

The sixth child is my throat and the seventh is yet to come.

At the age of seven, a girl might devote her life to perpetual virginity. A boy might put his second foot into purgatory.

It is the beginning of the age of reason and if a child has been taught by Jesuits, at the age of seven he will belong to the church forever.

If she has been taught by nature, she will be wild and happy forever.

☟

Are we in for a surprise?

The future is like magic. It wears no robes or veils but arrives naked, tossing its surprises to the right and the left. How does it arrive? It neither comes from ahead nor do we enter it running. This is because it and we can only approach what is always coming toward it and us. There is no possible action or sound that can be made without being received elsewhere, thereby describing and deciding the future, which only wears the attributes of something recognized as past.

Is there such a thing as truth objectively speaking? This question curves around and demands that I ask myself why I am asking the question in the first place, what good an answer will do for me before I am annihilated. If I am convinced that the story of your life and thought reveals the truth about our condition on this planet, then will I be happier as I proceed? Why else am I asking it?

≱

While I am still alive, going to work always feels brand new, like diving off a very high board into a stone-riddled ocean. I am never able to predict what will happen. Once I am there, with my students, time becomes self-contained within the four walls of the room. There seems to be no future.
Martin Buber said, "Good is direction and what is done in it."

I always tried to keep the classroom an egalitarian space with no competition allowed in. I tried, especially as I grew older, to lead them to the source of their work and to locate where its resolution might lie.

I wanted my students to deepen their own measure of themselves, using their stories or poems as others might yoga.

In some classes I made my students write children's stories to get them back to the source of the story as a form, to relearn the archetypes, to find the basic plots that suffuse all works of fiction, to use objects carefully, and only a few, to write in short purposeful sentences. I helped them study the ethical problems that are generated in simple terms in children's stories. The old stories by Grimm, Perrault, Andersen, Wilde—these were my chosen few to start with. Then, later, newer stories like *The Little House, The Little Engine That Could, Mike Mulligan, The Story of Ferdinand*—and *Rock Crystal* by Adalbert Stifter.

Sometimes when I taught, I felt as if I were planting an apple orchard in the rubbery char of Ground Zero because I still loved a

country trail and did not believe in the unconscious but in correspondences. This made me old-fashioned.

Why write if it is not to align yourself with time and space?
Better to wash the bottoms of the ill or dying. Better to have no
vacillating in your heart or mind, as Emerson recommends, and
to participate in what he calls abandonment.

"Only the act remains, unbound, absolute. It fuses subjects seeing and objects seen, into itself," Michel de Certeau wrote in his
poetic essay "White Ecstasy."

⚜

One night I dreamed I was writing a play and in it my students
were looking up at me with the blurry eyes of young sheep
and/or addicts of sex and drugs. Behind me there was a large
mountain with flags blowing there. And horses stood ready to
climb . . . no, not just to climb, but to race to the top, driven by
each one of the students who wanted to be first to touch a flag.
We couldn't tell which flag was closest, because of the distance,
but three set forth with charging ambition.

One held the horse too tight, another too loose, and a third found
herself on a horse that could not climb. The first was bucked off.
The second was taken on a wild ride. The third found herself
seated on a sitting horse. Up above the flags were flapping in
streaks of hard wind.

And two more students volunteered to climb on foot. They
reached the top, and somehow I was there beside them, but the
flags had blown away and so there was no way to know who was
a winner, who was not.

Around us lay heaps and humps of mountain ranges, brown and white, and streaked with rocklike plants. The wind still whirled around our faces. All their work had no meaning, without markers and prizes. Not just their work. Their lives seemed futile. Our lineaments were transparent and so were our skins.

The two students had what they called "panic attacks" and begged me to tell them: What is life worth living for?
Unfortunately I woke up in my sheets and could not send my message back to the world of dreams. My poor students! What could I have told them too late?

⚕

Yeats said he believed "in what I must call the evocation of spirits, though I do not know what they are, in the power of creating magical illusions, in the visions of truth in the depths of the mind when the eyes are closed; and I believe in three doctrines, which have, as I think, been handed down from early times, and been the foundations of nearly all magical practices. These doctrines are—

(1) That the borders of our mind are ever shifting, and that many minds can flow into one another, as it were, and create or reveal a single mind, a single energy.
(2) That the borders of our memories are as shifting, and that our memories are a part of one great memory, the memory of Nature herself."

On Ascension Day in the middle of May 1999, I went on a retreat hoping for a revelation. I hoped that I would find better words for spiritual phenomena than I was finding in the Catholic Church during the Eucharistic prayer and the homilies. I prayed the doors of heaven would fly open and I would see at last; I prayed because I did not believe any of it would happen. The flights from London to Italy were delayed because of the bombing in Belgrade. It was reported that in Venice people actually felt the ground quiver from the explosions.

In Florence my companion was mugged by a group of teenage girls—"gypsies" waving and jabbing cardboard at us while one of them grabbed her purse and kept it.
Marauding hordes of tourists angrily waited in long lines to see artworks and to eat.

Students were waving antiwar banners behind the Duomo. The city itself seemed defeated by engines and their human drivers, but both the students rebelling and the artwork offered some signs of resistance to bad progress.

The Villa San Leonardo al Palco (a former Franciscan monastery) sat high on a winding hill inside a semicircle of hills, then out across Prato, an orange-roofed, steamy little suburb. The gardens were a maze of high hedges dotted by rose bushes of all colors and species, and their fragrance permeated all of the three days.
Our rooms were clean cells with a variety of views.

We ate sometimes in silence, sometimes boisterously in a cool refectory where we were served Tuscan soups, bread, wine, cheeses, pasta. There were at least five hours of meditation each day, with about sixty people facing the chapel altar, a huge wooden crucifix, two meditation pillows, candles, the Benedictine Laurence Freeman and the Dalai Lama, who had organized this dialogue.

We got up early and went to bed around ten. Most everyone for those days spoke of a kind of brain buzz that was like a "strobe light effect," but no one could sleep.

It was a silent retreat with whispered encounters on balconies and in the gardens. Each morning we were led on a mindfulness meditation through the wet dewy hedges.

One day it rained, but most of the time there was a dull sun. Birds, roosters, a dog barking, farm machines buzzing, scooters, and horns honking around the twisting stone-walled streets and bells, bells, bells.

The Dalai Lama left twice for very short periods, accompanied by police and a helicopter that signaled his return. For the better part of the time we were all confined to the monastery, and no one was allowed in.

The buzz of the helicopter reminded us all of the war outside the walls of the monastery. And as usual I was distressed by the assumption that the only way to come face to face with the truth is by fasting, meditating, practicing compassion and altruism, and entering a cell. Isn't it possible that those are conscious disciplines for a few people that most others suffer in the course of an ordinary day: being hungry, getting high, crying out to God, being lonely, fair, generous, and full of pity for others?

⚘

There were two dialogue sessions when the Dalai Lama and Laurence Freeman talked, each in turn, and His Holiness through a translator.

The first morning the subject was scripture; the second morning it was image.

In the afternoon, the participants were given time to ask questions, and then we met in small groups for conversation and to prepare one collective question for the Dalai Lama.

Many of the questions seemed to involve the problem of suffering as the presence of Kosovo and an occupied Tibet loomed large.

Many of the participants were Buddhist practitioners and many were Christians who had been practicing meditation. The Dalai Lama taught us Tonglen meditation, which is focused on suffering and liberation from it, and he directed a Buddhist ceremony at one of the afternoon meetings; later he gave the homily on loving others.

"Don't talk. Act," he stressed.

He confessed that he didn't know for sure, but he believed that prayer did nothing for anyone else, especially in political or wartime situations, unless perhaps a person was praying for someone very close to her, like a child or other family member.

He kept insisting that one could become deeper through prayer and meditation, but it should not be used it as a substitute for other-directed action. He was very empirical, very practical, yet he said that he used divination and dreams to help him make decisions after he had already consulted with others and thought things through himself.

Being there was like wandering through an atmosphere far above sea level or visiting a dream to which you knew you could never return. The snowy whiteness of the English Benedictine beside the maroon-robed Buddhist intensified the sense of being in a symbolic dream system.

While the Dalai Lama made it clear that he believed that people should first learn their own religious tradition in depth, he was convinced that meditation would deepen their understanding and practice of it and help them to serve the suffering world.

He was glad to explain Buddhism, and to share some of the rituals (pinches of rice falling like rain during a rite for generosity), but it was clear that the reason he was involved in this whole enterprise was not to win converts to Buddhism but to encourage Christians to be more Christlike in the service of world peace.

There are "parallels," he admitted, between Christianity and Buddhism, but the two are fundamentally separated over the question of God.

In response Freeman didn't do the usual thing and give attributes to God or get into the architecture of the Trinity. Instead, he showed how the Catholic tradition aspired to nondualism. The Dalai Lama seemed heartened by this, but not entirely convinced.

All this time I hoped that they would not be able to sense my bitterness, exhaustion, lack of hope, critical witnessing of others, my inability to concentrate or meditate, the way my mind raced, my selfishness, my excess reserve. I prayed they would not sense or see me at all. Buddhists like school and I don't. They have lessons for everything and they enjoy sitting in the position of students, learning how to interpret their own gestures.

The next lesson we discussed was the Christian idea of mercy. "Mercy" was presented as a radical concept closer to the Buddhist word *compassion* than to the Christian word *love.*
And now, surprisingly, a woman was introduced as the image of compassion and an object of the Dalai Lama's greatest admiration. Mary! He didn't make fun of her apparitions but believed that they had really occurred and that she was sending us im-

portant messages about the necessity for peace. She was, in a very real way, the Christian Buddha, and he was perplexed by her removal from Protestant churches.

At one point the term *highest values* came into the conversation as the common denominator for every civilization—what we all could agree on (for instance, the desire for happiness)—when talk of God fell flat (as it should). The two monks wanted to articulate the highest values from two entirely different cultural bases and to see if they converged.

The Dalai Lama repeated his conviction that the only way to end mental and emotional affliction was through altruism and the practice of service to others. What he liked best about Jesus was his self-sacrificing action (kenosis). Again he said that meditation was service to oneself in order to serve others, a kind of recharging of the batteries.

Through meditation and prayer one should continually aspire to altruism by envisioning all human suffering present in every person and society; and by altruism he meant the continual active practice of putting others before oneself.

On the last morning, he reiterated his point about the importance of adhering, if possible, to your own religious tradition. Why? Because each religion has at its heart the same message about altruism. Therefore, nothing could be more valuable than to crack open and rediscover the tradition that you already understand, in order to find convergence points with others.

He loved teaching Buddhism to others, because it contributed to this deepening and merging. Originally he was drawn to Christianity because of the Catholic aid workers who helped the Tibetan people in India at the onset of their diaspora. In their generous action he envisioned the potential for a world peace movement that was based in tolerance toward other religions and philosophies.

A Tibetan hymn was read aloud by the translator, begging Buddha not to enter Nirvana and leave the suffering world behind.

At the end of the program we all gathered in a huge outdoor circle for our good-byes and photographs, and the Dalai Lama walked over and selected my arm to hold.

The Chosen

To be chosen can be good or bad.

The body of a deer, slung over a tree, frozen, taught me this lesson.

Being is an enclosure like any other.

The senses form a case around the interior.

Being can be demolished in one blow.

The enclosure disintegrates, falls, and leaves the interior open to air.

Then being becomes what we call spirit, because it participates no longer in the senses that enclosed it. They drop back to earth.

Being's breath returns to what we call the void, which is the water of the universe, but is its own spirit.

When being is an enclosure it moves from point to point.

A tree exists but it doesn't "be" because it can't lift its trunk and roots and move voluntarily.

Yes, being must hurt more than a tree does. Maybe not!

Tears are the sign of its participation in pain. Tears are sometimes considered a sacrament and caught and kept in little jars.

Then you can bless someone with these tears. They are the mark of being in suffering.

They are evidence of the incarnate nature of sadness and the senses.

A baby's tears are most potent as a blessing, holy water.

Like dry mustard or venison, the parts of being have no beauty when severed from their source.

Being is either a reflection of the world outside it, a weaving into that world, or a wandering reflector from which images bounce off and back.

These three relationships are in constant flux. This makes them beautiful, because what is both cold and fleeting is poetry.

Being is physically related to time, breath is the evidence for this.

Breath and its pulse.
When the spirit brooded over the waters, the spirit was time's
consciousness. It still is.

When time is conscious, it is the spirit brooding.

Consciousness like most things has layers. The first layer circles
the hair; it might even be the hair.
The next layer dissolves into an area that goes as far as the horizon (for an eye, the horizon is what can be seen; for an ear it's
what can be heard).
This layer is depicted as a halo in paint.
The third layer is where the ethereal beings dwell.
This layer of consciousness is mistakenly called "the word" in
the sense of scripture, language. It has devolved over the course
of centuries into the wrong meaning.

It represents all infused meanings and expressions, including
music, poetry, dance, art, math, physics, philosophy—these forms
that shoot themselves toward the upper layer, like darts on a
target.
You try to hit consciousness to see if it is there.
It is there watching like a stag when its neck is turned and it sees
what it fears.

Once I hunted a person like an animal. Then he turned to look
at me with such terror, I dropped my arrows and never picked
them up again.
I realized I had turned into a hunter who blames the hunted for
not allowing itself to be caught.
The animal was Brahman.

The Land of Dreams

In the old days the people maintained that all produce was traded based on use and not on gain. Sugar for rice. Wheat for tools, linen, tobacco, hides, and tea. White honey was freely given by the bees and made into consecrated wax for the altar.

When people sang, the Jesuits and the Sisters of the Sacred Heart sang along. The orchids ripened from the sound. All this was in another time that is still standing somewhere.

This is why, once in a while, I always pity prayer that has such a long way to go.

For instance when one-eyed Jesus went out to pray, the other children followed him. He fell in the water and drowned, and they all jumped in to save him. What happened to him? He broke into billions.

His prayer? Who knows.

On another day, which was really night, because every day is in darkness, Jesus went out to play and the other children chased him over the bridge of a sunbeam. They fell into the water and drowned. What happened to Jesus? He multiplied. And the name of the stick that brought him down was God.

Cataracts poured into a river five miles in breadth, circular eddies twirled like pinwheels.
Monkeys turned whips into toys and parrots mimicked the pop of bubbles until coins were formed by minerals.
The sunbeam fell and spattered into orbs.
Fish slapped the pink surface of dawn.

All this was like Jesus after the Jesuits and the Sisters were in bed and after the sky was a shadow and no one believed in anything but dreams and stories like the one about a man on a road striding up a hill and then after, at a table, laughing and being now a new person in a new form though they recognized him.

For we gather and discard simultaneously as we move in time. It makes life hard to understand and put in perspective. Only recognition can serve us to the end.

Now Jesus shimmers in other bodies, Jesus the boy born with black eyes, Jesus the girl born laughing to the left, the little one with his red mouth, the two at either ear, cherubs tipped and listening. It is the baby of the throat calling out.

"Charity is the root and foundation of our lives," say the Sisters who have seen what this means.

Evocation

Once I was a child.

I am sure of this, more sure than I am that I raised my own children; or that those long difficult days really happened; or that I paid for each day and we got through them alive. My childhood is fixed as if inside a colorful book, its atmosphere strong, full of pictures as solid as planets. I carry my fear of losing it around with me; it can only feel safe when other, living children are near.

The last trip for a job I once had was to meet a woman I had met (before I had begun the job) who would now be replacing me at it.

I hauled myself to Amsterdam with a three-day train-boat trip from London to Paris in six hours without leaving the ground and reading about Ramakrishna.

The day in Paris was warm and sunny, the air soft, the fleshy walls of buildings bent toward each other. I was in Le Marais with its high double windows holding in the lights where I sat with my notebook outdoors in a courtyard. Night walk along the boulevard du Temple. And the next two days were spent in warm misty weather, leaves yellow, shells of chestnuts cracked and flattened, wheat-colored buildings, and nights in the Hotel Unic after long, long walking and brooding.

Loneliness and yearning are often mistaken for each other.

Thanksgiving gray, chilly, a light snow on the fields from Boulogne down—the whiteness of the statues in the Tuileries.

There are the little white roses of Renoir in the Orangerie.
And that hotel near Saint-Julien-le-Pauvre.
Flew through the Egyptian adobe of the Louvre,
Views shone out around the dusk,
Where flames flew off the carousel and twigs were white.

Stumpy trees with elegant laced twigs.
In back of some benches down an alley of winter trees—
This is one way to meet oneself coming the other way.
How the objects have acquired layers of association
With their repetition through the years,
Making each sense-experience more poignant,
Almost unbearably bright, sharp, an unexpected surplus value
Acquired by the luck of living so long.
Sterling silver twigs in the late evening.

⚑

The slack woman was sitting at a table under an old striped umbrella that looked as if it were designed in 1940. It was cold. We both drank cognac with rock sugar dropped into it. I recognized her as someone whose mother had survived Buchenwald. Once she had told me that her mother suspected everyone she met of being a potential collaborator or whore to the SS.

"Everyone?" I had asked.
"The only people she loved were people who would not have lasted."
"Are you still depressed?" I asked her now.
"Because I have survived my mother's disapproval, no," she said.
"Will you be able to go on and become a productive member of the company?"
"The ones who are angriest are most useful," she replied.
"They get it out of their system?"
"They put it into the system."

Her hands were veined and wrinkled, rings on two fingers must have become embedded in the bones by now. Her eyes had my father's intensity, but she was not American and spoke with the insistence of one at a distance.

She said: "You are welcome to commit suicide. Everyone is. I am with the existentialists on this point. If the State is contemptuous of the old, the ill, the mentally deranged, the weak, then they have good reason to commit suicide. If you are neglected and anonymous, you have the right to take your own life. There are slow suicides through misery, narcotics, alcohol and fast ones off bridges and ceilings. Suicide bombers don't want to live anymore, they want to go to Paradise at once, but do they get there? Who knows. Even Moses. . . . You can always sacrifice yourself for a cause, do something that will kill you and save someone else. This is good suicide."

"I wasn't thinking of all that," I told her, "but I am glad to have your opinion."
"You are suffering from the empty nest," she told me. "I can see it in your body and on your face. No wonder. You know that no one but children will ever love you again."

Surprised, I stood up. "Run away, that's good," she said. "That's the way you'll adapt to the next stage. You might even help create it. Do you remember Mayakovsky's poem?

> Roses and dreams
> debased by poets
> will unfold
> in a new light
> for the delight of our eyes
> the eyes of big children.
> We will invent new roses
> Roses of capitals with petals of squares.

I said I did remember it. She told me to "go on then" and "take care of the children." So I left her with instructions for her job and headed west to collect my nomadic group.

⚇

A day later the children handed me a cloth bag and some shoes
I left behind in Caen.
Then they ran up and down the stairs of the narrow hotel
Making friends with the cleaning ladies
Who couldn't understand their English.
Some gave them sweets to eat.
The snow spread over the little city turrets
While I told them the story of Hans Christian Andersen.
I said that whatever he described as terrible was what he loved
most about life.
The yellow interiors of shops were like perfume bottles in
Candlelight.
We took up our instruments: book, pen, paper, passports, and
Tickets.
And set off on the first lap of our trip to Ireland.
Although the children were hungry by then
They could only agree on baguettes and apples.
So I sat down, drank wine, and watched them eat.

References

The Further Shore by Abishiktananda

Killer of Sheep, a movie by Charles Burnett

The Mountain of the Women by Liam Clancy

Sphota Theory of Lanugauge by Harold C. Coward

The Possession at Loudun by Michel de Certeau

The Mystic Fable by Michel de Certeau

The Cave of the Heart by Shirley du Boulay

Hindu Manners, Customs and Ceremonies
   by Abbé J. A. Dubois

For Love of Insects by Thomas Eisner

Nights of Cabiria, a movie by Fedrico Fellini

Sankaracarya's Concept of Relation by Sara Grant

Toward an Alternative Theology by Sara Grant

Lord of the Dance by Sara Grant

The Europeans by Henry James

And There Was Light by Jacques Lusseyran

Mount Venus by Mary Manning

Look Back in Anger,
   a movie by John Osborne and Tony Richardson

Luther, a play by John Osborne

Dictionary of Theology by Karl Rahner

Star of Redemption by Franz Rosenzweig

The Devils, a movie by Ken Russell

Lectures on Philosophy by Simone Weil

Frost in May by Antonia White

As Once in May by Antonia White

Some of these pieces have appeared in *Mantis,* the *Tyrant, Janus Head, Conjunctions,* the *New England Journal of Public Policy,* the *Poker, Carnet de Route,* the *Denver Quarterly, War and Peace,* the Poetry Foundation web site, and *Religion and the Arts* (Boston College). I am very grateful to the editors who took them.

And I heartily thank the John Simon Guggenheim Foundation, the Bellagio Foundation, the Studium and Sisters of the Order of St. Benedict, Glenstal Abbey, and the Lannan Foundation at Marfa, Texas, for their support during the writing of this book. Special gratitude goes to my editors Fiona McCrae, Jeffrey Shotts, and Katie Dublinski, and to Professor Royal Rhodes at Kenyon College, to Mark Conway, Susan Moon, Dunstan Morrissey, and to Richard and Anne Kearney in Southwest Cork.

Fanny Howe is the author of more than thirty books of poetry and prose, including *Second Childhood,* a finalist for the National Book Award, and *The Needle's Eye: Passing through Youth.* She has won the Lenore Marshall Poetry Prize, a fellowship from the Guggenheim Foundation, an award from the American Academy of Arts and Letters, the Gold Medal for Poetry from the Commonwealth Club of California, and the Ruth Lilly Poetry Prize for lifetime achievement from the Poetry Foundation. Howe was a finalist for the International Man Booker International Prize for her fiction. She lives in New England.